THE TWOFOLD LIFE

OR

CHRIST'S WORK FOR US

—————— AND ——————

CHRIST'S WORK IN US

BY

A. J. GORDON, D.D.

HODDER AND STOUGHTON
LONDON MCMX

Printed by Hazell, Watson & Viney, Ld., London and Aylesbury.

CONTENTS.

IX.

X.

XI.

LIFE AND LIFE MORE ABUNDANT.

"The work of Jesus in the world is two-fold. It is a work accomplished *for us*, destined to effect *reconciliation* between God and man ; it is a work accomplished *in us*, with the object of effecting our *sanctification*. By the one, a right relation is established between God and us ; by the other is the *fruit* of the re-established order. By the former the condemned sinner is received into the state of grace ; by the latter the pardoned sinner is associated with the life of God. . . . How many express themselves as if when forgiveness, with the peace which it procures, has been once obtained, all is finished, and the work of salvation complete. They seem to have no suspicion that salvation consists in the health of the soul, and that the health of the soul consists in holiness. Forgiveness is not the re-establishment of health, it is but the crisis of convalescence. If God thinks fit to declare the sinner righteous, it is in order that He may by that means restore him to holiness."—*Godet*.

I.

LIFE AND LIFE MORE ABUNDANT

INTRODUCTORY.

IT is an unhappy circumstance that so many Christians look upon the salvation of the soul as the goal rather than as the starting-point of faith. We do not forget, indeed, that the Scripture uses the expression " receiving *the end of your faith,* even the salvation of your souls." But the connection clearly shows that it is the further end, not the nearer end which is here referred to, the perfecting and glorifying of the soul at the revelation of Jesus Christ, not its justification when it believes on Christ. " He that believeth on the Son *hath* eternal life "—has it in germ and principle. But Christ says, " I am come that they might have life, *and that they might have it more abundantly.*"* Christ for us, appropriated by faith, is the source of life ; Christ within us through the indwelling of the Holy Spirit is the source of more abundant life ; the one fact secures our salvation ; the other enables us to glorify God in the salvation

---

* John x. 10.

1

of others. How distinctly these two stages of
spiritual life are set forth in our Lord's discourse
about the water of life! The first effect upon the
believer of drinking this water is, "he shall never
thirst : but the water that I shall give him shall be
in him a well of water springing up into everlasting
life."* That is, the soul receives salvation, and the
perennial joy and peace which accompany salvation.
But the second stage is this : " He that believeth on
me, as the Scripture hath said, out of his belly shall
flow rivers of living water. *But this spake He of the
Spirit which they that believe on Him should receive.*"†
Here is the divine life going out in service and
testimony and blessing through the Holy Ghost.

It is the last stage, the fulness and consequent
outgiving of the influences of the Spirit, which needs
to be especially sought in these days by Christians.
There are so many instances of arrested development in the Church; believers who have settled into
a condition of confirmed infancy, and whose testimony always begins back with conversion, and
hovers around that event, like the talk of children
who are perpetually telling how old they are. Now
even our conversion, blessed event as it is, may be
one of those things that are behind, which we are to
forget in the pursuit of higher things. Is there not
a deep significance in that expression of two-fold
union which our Lord so often uses, " Ye in Me and
I in you "? The branch that is in the vine has its

---

* John iv. 14   † John vii. 38, 39.

position ; but only as the vine is in it, constantly penetrating it with its sap and substance, does it have power for fruitfulness. "*If any man be in Christ* he is a new creature," he is regenerated, he is justified. But what, let us inquire, can the apostle's words mean when in referring to such regenerated ones he says, " My little children, *of whom I travail in birth again until Christ be formed in you*" ?*
This later travail—these second birth-pangs for those who had already been born of the Spirit— what can they signify ? Is it metaphor, or is it a hint of some deeper work of divine renewing for those who, having begun in the Spirit, are in danger of seeking to be made perfect in the flesh ?

Now the Scriptures seem to teach that there is a second stage in spiritual development, distinct and separate from conversion ; sometimes widely separated in time from it, and sometimes almost contemporaneous with it—a stage to which we rise by a special renewal of the Holy Ghost, and not merely by the process of gradual growth. We shall be especially careful not to dogmatize here. But there is a transaction described in the New Testament by the terms the gift of the Holy Ghost, the sealing of the Spirit, the anointing of the Holy Spirit, and the like. The allusions to it in the Acts and in the Epistles mark it unmistakably as something different from conversion. What is this experience ? We take our place as learners, before the Scriptures and

* Gal. iv. 19.

before the biographies of holy men, and seek an answer to this inquiry.

We come to this study under two impulses. The one has been derived from a fresh study of the Acts of the Apostles, and from the conviction begotten by such study that there is more light to break out of that book than we have yet imprisoned in our creeds ; the other has been derived from new experience in revival work, and from the observation of what great things the Spirit of God can still accomplish when He falls upon believers and fills them with His power.

Here is the lesson, above all others, which this generation needs to learn. Do we mourn that ours is a materialistic age ? Would that it were only so on the scientific and rationalistic side. But what we have most reason to fear is that subtle material-ism which is creeping into our church life and methods. How little dependence is there on super-natural power as all-sufficient for our work ! How much we are coming to lean on mere human agencies !—upon art and architecture, upon music and rhetoric and social attraction ! If we would draw the people to church that we may win them to Christ, the first question with scores of Christians nowadays is, What new turn can be given to the kaleidoscope of entertainment ? What new stop can we insert in our organ, and what richer and more exquisite strain can we reach by our quartette ? What fresh novelty in the way of social attraction

can we introduce ; or what new corruscation can be
let off from the pulpit to dazzle and captivate the
people ? Oh for a faith to abandon utterly these
devices of naturalism, and to throw the Church
without reserve upon the power of the supernatural !
Is there not some higher degree in the Holy Spirit's
tuition into which we can graduate our young
ministers, instead of sending them to a German
university for their last touches of theological
culture ? Is there not some reserved power yet
treasured up in the Church which is the Body of
Christ, some unknown or neglected spiritual force
which we can lay hold of, and so get courage to
fling away for ever these frivolous expedients on
which we have so much relied for carrying on the
Lord's work ? The enduement of the Spirit for
power, for service, for testimony, for success—this,
in brief, is the subject of this book.

That we might set the matter most effectively
before our readers, we have adopted the following
method :

1. First, we have considered the subject under
the head of " the two-fold life," in order to mark
clearly the distinctions between the first and the
second stages of spiritual experience. For one of
the most serious mistakes touching the whole
matter, has been the habit of confounding what
belongs to sanctification with what really belongs to
justification, and *vice versâ.* It is very common,
for example, to find writers on the Higher Christian

life urging us to become " completely crucified with Christ," and "utterly dead to sin." But these are not experiences or attainments ; they are fundamental facts. The Revised New Testament throws a flood of light on this point, by putting all allusions to the believer's death with Christ, in the past definite tense where they belong. It is simply a fact that when Christ our substitute died on the cross for us, we died virtually or judicially through Him to the law and to sin. As saith the Scripture, " If One died for all, *then all died.*"* It is this past definite transaction which forms the basis of our acceptance with God. " He that hath died is justified from sin."† Here is something that has to do directly with our justification by faith, and not with our sanctification by the Spirit.

On the other hand, the error has sometimes been committed of insisting on the higher spiritual experiences as an evidence of conversion ; the witness of the Spirit and the sealing of the Spirit being demanded as prerequisite to baptism and admission to the Church. A glance at the Acts of the Apostles shows us that it was not so in the beginning. The record of the first admissions to the Church is very simple. " Then they that gladly received the word were baptized." A consent of the heart to Christ and to His gospel was the solitary condition of initiation into the Church and the deeper operations of the Holy Ghost followed in their order.

* 2 Cor. v. 14.   † Rom. vi. 7 ; Rev. Ver.

In what we have written we have given far larger space to the second stage of the two-fold life, but we have brought it into constant contrast with the first, in order to emphasize these distinctions and set them clearly before the mind.

2. We have endeavoured to throw all possible light on this subject from the records of Christian experience. It is evident, if we stop to think of the matter, that the Spirit must be studied in His operations. The fault of most treatises on the Third Person of the Trinity is that they are too abstract. A spirit can only be made known to us by his outward acts and manifestations. Our Lord hints this in His simile of the wind blowing where it listeth. We can see the swaying of the trees and the heaving of the waters, but we cannot discern the wind that causeth these motions. So we can see the power of the Holy Ghost in the lives of Christians, in conversions and revivals ; in the acts of believers and in the triumphs of the Church ; but we cannot recognize Him by Himself, since He is invisible and immaterial. Why is it that the Acts of the Apostles gives us so much knowledge of the Holy Ghost ? Because it is the life of the Spirit seen in the words and deeds of the body of believers : it is the Invisible made visible in working and conduct and testimony. Indeed, the Acts of the Apostles might be rightly named the Acts of the Holy Spirit. As the Gospels are a record " of all that Jesus began both to do and teach until the day in which He was taken up," so

the Acts are the record of all that the Holy Spirit began both to do and teach after that He came down and inhabited the body of the faithful. And if we learn so much from these first beginnings of His working, is there not much to learn from His continuings in the subsequent history of the Church ?

We judge so ; and hence we have called to our aid the lives of the saints of all the Christian ages. Having drawn our scheme of the doctrine of the Spirit from the Scriptures, we have sought to fill up the outline from the records of religious biography. For Christian experience, if it be true and divinely inspired, is but the Bible translated and printed in illuminated text, scripture "writ large," for the benefit of dim eyes that cannot read the fine print of doctrine. Let our readers judge for themselves of the significance of the spiritual transactions herein recorded.

3. Finally, in all that we have written we have had chiefly in mind the help and quickening of Christian ministers and workers. No elaborate treatise has been attempted ; no exhaustive discussion of the person and ministry of the Holy Spirit. Rather have we attempted an easy colloquy with our readers, blending Scripture exposition with religious incident, letting the voice of God be heard now in His inspired Word, and now in the echoes which that Word has awakened in Christian consciousness. And upon all, we have sought, and do now seek, the illuminating and sanctifying and

consecrating influences of the Holy Paraclete—that what in our discourse is true and according to the mind of God may be blessed to His people ; and that whatever is amiss may be graciously forgiven and overruled.

REGENERATION AND RENEWAL.

" By regeneration we understand the commencement of the life of God in the soul of man ; *the beginning of that which had not an existence before :* by renewal, the invigoration of that which has been begun ; the sustentation of a life already possessed. . . . In the washing of regeneration the new life commences. Having begun, it needs to be supported and preserved. This is effected by the renewing of the Holy Ghost, the flowing into the soul through the supply of the Spirit of Jesus Christ of the varied gifts of the Divine Agent by whom the life itself was imparted at first."—*Thomas Binney.*

II.

REGENERATION AND RENEWAL.

REGENERATION and Renewal are related to each other as the planting of the tree is related to its growth. It is very necessary that at the outset we should have a clear conception of what regeneration is. In the manuals of theology we sometimes find it described as "a change of nature." But we must take respectful exception to this definition. For by nature must be meant, of course, human nature ; and by the expression " change of nature," it is implied that the natural heart can be so transformed and bettered, that it can bring forth the fruits of righteousness and true holiness. Against this presumption the Word of God enters its solemn and emphatic caveat—" Because the carnal mind is enmity against God : for it is not subject to the law of God, *neither indeed can be.*" *

We hold that the true definition of regeneration is, that it is "the communication of the Divine Nature to man by the operation of the Holy Spirit, through the word." So writes the Apostle Peter : " Whereby are given unto us exceeding great and

---

* Rom. viii. 7.

precious promises ; that by these we might be *partakers of the divine nature,* having escaped the corruption that is in the world through lust." * As Christ was made partaker of human nature by His incarnation, that so He might enter into truest fellowship with us, we are made partakers of the Divine Nature by regeneration, that we may enter into truest fellowship with God. That great saying of the Son of God which is so often repeated in the Gospel and Epistles of John, " He that believeth on Me hath eternal life," can convey to us only this idea when rightly understood. The eternal life is not our natural life prolonged into endless duration. It is the divine life imparted to us—the very life of very God communicated to the human soul, and bringing forth there its own proper fruit.

Seeing this point clearly, we can readily understand the process and method of spiritual growth— that it consists in the constant mortification of the natural man, and the constant renewal of the spiritual man. We can best illustrate this by using the figure of grafting, which the Scriptures several times employ. Here is a gnarly tree, which bears only sour and stunted fruit. From some rich and perfect stock a scion is brought, which is incorporated into a branch of this tree. Now, the husbandman's efforts are directed, not to the culture and improvement of the old stock, but to the development of the new. Instead of seeking to make the original

* 2 Peter i. 4.

branches better, he cuts them off, here and there, that the sap and vitality which they are wasting in the production of worthless fruit may go to that which is approved and excellent. Here is the philosophy of spiritual culture : " Put off the *old man* with his deeds " ; " the *inward man* is renewed day by day."

Believing that vigilant and serious attention to spiritual culture is now especially demanded, if we are to cope with the powerful enemies which confront us, let us search for the secret of this divine renewal.

"*Day by day*" our inward man is renewed. " Give us *day by day* our daily bread," is the prayer which the Saviour taught us to utter. And yet He said, " It is written that man shall not live by bread alone, but by every word that proceedeth out of the mouth of God." The bread of the Word is that which we must feed upon if we would enjoy a daily increase in the life of God. It is a trite admonition, but none the less true and vital. Divine growth must follow the development of the divine birth. If we were " begotten by the Word of Truth," we must be daily renewed from the same element.

Too few really credit the power of the Word in building up holy character, and, therefore, too few make diligent experiment of the process. Can we think it possible that the food on our tables should be so transmuted in Nature's laboratory that it should reappear, now in the stalwart muscle of the

blacksmith's arm, and now in the fine texture of the
poet's brain ?   And let it not seem incredible that
the Word of God, daily received and inwardly assimilated, can reappear in every kind of spiritual power
and holy efficiency.   Stephen Grellet, waking up
from his early sacramental training, saw the washer-
women one day at their tasks.   They were washing
linen.   He says : " I wondered to see what beating
and pounding there was upon it, and how beautifully white it came out of their hands.   I was told I
could not enter God's kingdom until I underwent
such an operation ; that unless I was thus washed
and made white, I could have no part in the dear
Son of God.   For weeks I was absorbed in the consideration of the subject—the washing of regeneration.   I had never heard such things before, and I
greatly wondered that, having been baptized with
water, and having also received what they call the
sacrament of confirmation, I should have to pass
through such a purification."   Just as it was in the
beginning, we see, " How shall ye believe if I tell
you of heavenly things ? "

But by-and-by this mystery is solved, by being
wrought out in a living personal experience, and the
regeneration of the Spirit is followed by a long life
of eager and humble feeding on the Spirit and the
Word of God.   And now appears a greater mystery.
By a strange and subtle power the hearts of kings
and emperors are made to open to this saintly
preacher, while they listen entranced as he unfolds to

them the mysteries of the kingdom of heaven, and pleads the claims of Divine Love. Popes and cardinals, priests and nuns, give ear ; their hearts melt, and their eyes flow with tears, while they confess that they never heard it on this wise before. Here is a life which maintained such communion with God, that there was far more of heaven than of earth in it. Let us see in it a living testimony of what the Holy Spirit and the Holy Word can effect when wrought into living Christian character.

We are touching a most vital point now. Physiology shows us how inevitably the food on which one subsists determines the texture of his flesh. Can the daily newspaper, the light romance, and the secular magazine, build up the fibre and tissue of a true spiritual character? We are not putting any surly prohibition on these things ; but when we think of the place which they hold in modern society, and with how many Christians they constitute the larger share of the daily reading, there is suggested a very serious theme for reflection. As the solemn necessity is laid upon the sinner of choosing between Christ and the world, so is the choice pressed upon the Christian between the Bible and literature—that is, the choice as to which shall hold the supreme place. " Blessed are they that *hunger and thirst after righteousness.*" Ah! how quickly a day's bodily languor and want of appetite is noted and attended to. But how many days have we known in which there has been no relish for the Word of

God, no deep, inward craving after that meat which
the world knows not of. And have we been so
alarmed at this symptom that we have made haste
at once to seek its cure ?

The fact of the Scriptures furnishing nutriment
and upbuilding to the soul, is the most real experience of which we have knowledge. None of us
"*by taking thought*, can add one cubit unto his
stature." But how many, by taking in God's great
thoughts, feeding on them and inwardly digesting
them, have added vastly to their spiritual stature.
We have noticed especially, in the lives of Christians,
how some long-neglected but freshly-revived truth
has marvellously quickened and built up the soul.
Its newness has created a strong relish in the
believer, and so imparted a mighty impulse to his
spiritual growth. How true this has been of such
doctrines as those of " Justification by Faith," " The
Witness of the Spirit," and the " Coming of the
Lord." The revival of these doctrines has constituted distinct eras of reformation in the Church, but
previously, also, marked eras of renewal in the
individual soul. We may take the last-mentioned
as the one most recently revived. The biographer
of Hewitson says of him : " He not only believed in
the speedy appearing, but loved it, waited for it,
watched for it. So mighty a motive power did it
become that he ever used to speak of it afterward
as bringing with it a kind of second conversion."
Yes ; and how many Christians of our day know

what this means!   Such is the vivifying power of
truth ; so does it come in to repair the waste in our
spiritual life, to build up new tissue, and to put new
blood into our heavenly man.

The same may be said of prayer and meditation.
They have mighty renewing power.   They quicken
our life, and multiply within us the joy of the Lord,
which is our strength.

In these days, when the closet has become so
contracted and the Church so expanded ; when
Christians have learned to find their edification so
largely in the public services, in the music, and art,
and eloquence of the sanctuary, and so little in
the still hour of communion, it is quite hard to
believe that the greatest enjoyment is possible in
solitude with God.   We read of Columkill bidding
farewell to his hermit's cell and homely fare to take
the honours and emoluments of the bishopric of Iona,
yet exclaiming tearfully : " Farewell, Arran of my
heart !   Paradise is with thee ; the garden of God
is within sound of thy bells."   And as we read this
we say, forsooth, " This is monkish sentimentalism."
But what when we find sober Protestant saints like
the one just quoted, Hewitson, writing : " Communion with Christ is the only source of satisfaction,
the only source of lasting joy.   I have enjoyed more
even this morning from beholding the loveliness of
the glory of Christ, as revealed to me by the Spirit,
than I have done from the world during the whole
of my life " ?   Or, to rise to a still more incredible

altitude, what if we listen to that mighty interceder
with God, John Welch, of Scotland, crying in one of
his seasons of rapt communion, "O Lord, hold Thy
hand ; it is enough ; Thy servant is a clay vessel,
and can contain no more " ?   Surely, this is strange
language to most of us.   But if we turn to the
Scriptures of our Lord, we may find a possible key
to such alleged experiences ; for when we ask our
Master why He has revealed such wonderful things
concerning our union with Him, and our share in the
Father's glory, He answers, "These things have I
spoken unto you that My joy might remain in you,
and *that your joy might be full.*"*   And when we
ask Him why He has given us this wonderful privi-·
lege of prayer in His name, He replies, " Ask and ye
shall receive, *that your joy may be full.*" †   If, at
best, we have been able to get only a half measure
of this divine joy, let us not discredit those who
have exclaimed, "*My cup runneth over.*   Surely
goodness and mercy shall follow me all the days of
my life."

We have spoken of daily renewals, and we are
persuaded that no real growth and development in
Christian life is possible without these.   There is
still another kind of renewing to which we would
call attention.   "*The times of refreshing from the
presence of the Lord,*" which the Scriptures promise,
hold out a very blessed and assuring hope.   This
expression, of course, has literal reference to the

---

* John xv. 11.   † John xvi. 24.

return of the Lord from glory, and His joyful reunion
with His Church. But there are even now seasons
of extraordinary communion with the Lord, when,
through the Holy Spirit, He is pleased to manifest
Himself to the soul in such unwonted power that
they may be truly called "times of refreshing."
We find records of these in the lives of almost all
devoted saints. As nature has its annual as well as
its diurnal renewals, when the sun returns in spring-tide
blessing and quickening, so has grace its special
times of revival. Then it is that the Heavenly Bride-
groom visits the soul, by the Holy Ghost, speaking
in tenderest accents : " Rise up, my love, my fair
one, and come away. For lo, the winter is past, the
rain is over and gone. The flowers appear on the
earth ; the time of the singing of birds is come, and
the voice of the turtle is heard in the land. The fig-
tree putteth forth her green figs, and the vines
with the tender grapes give a good smell. Arise,
my love, my fair one, and come away." Ah ! how
often have the poetic strains of this Song of Solomon
been translated into the real prose of living, practical
experience. The chill of winter has settled over
the Church ; instead of melting penitence, the tears
of other days have frozen into icicles, and are hang-
ing about the sanctuary—cold and glittering for-
malities taking the place of that holy tenderness
which pleads with God " with strong crying," and
warns men " night and day with tears." What
servant of God has not had sorrowful experiences of

this condition of things? Then it is that pastors
and brethren should seek for a special refreshing
from the Lord's presence. The ordinary tenor of
spiritual life will not answer now. The power of
God must be laid hold of—special power for special
weakness and need. And "blessed be the God and
Father of our Lord Jesus Christ, who hath begotten
us again unto a lively hope by the resurrection of
Jesus Christ from the dead," that He can renew what
he has begotten, and restore the joy of His salvation
to those who have backslidden into the joy of this
world. Christmas Evans, the fervent Welsh
preacher, has left us the record of a most gracious
visitation of this kind :—

"I was weary of a cold heart toward Christ and His
sacrifice and the work of His Spirit; of a cold heart in the
pulpit, in secret prayer, and in the study. For fifteen
years previously I had felt my heart burning within me,
as if going to Emmaus with Jesus. On a day ever to be
remembered by me, as I was going from Dolgelley to
Machynlleth, and climbing up toward Cadair Idris, I considered it incumbent on me to pray, however hard I felt
my heart, and however worldly the frame of my spirit was.
Having began in the name of Jesus, I soon felt, as it were,
the fetters loosening, and the old hardness softening, and,
as I thought, the mountains of frost and snow dissolving
and melting within me. This engendered confidence in
my soul in the promise of the Holy Ghost. I felt my
whole mind relieved from some great bondage; tears
flowed copiously, and I was constrained to cry out for the
gracious visits of God, by restoring to my soul the joy of
His salvation, and that He would visit the churches in

Anglesea that were under my care. I embraced in my supplications all the churches of the saints, and nearly all the ministers of the principality by their names. This struggle lasted for three hours; it rose again and again, like one wave after another, or a high-flowing tide driven by a strong wind, until my nature became faint by weeping and crying. Thus I resigned myself to Christ, body and soul, gifts and labours, all my life—every day and every hour that remained for me ; and all my cares I committed to Christ. The road was mountainous and lonely, and I was wholly alone, and suffered no interruption in my wrestling with God. From this time I was led to expect the goodness of God to the churches and to myself. . . . The result was, when I returned home the first thing that arrested my attention was that the Spirit was working also in the brethren in Anglesea, inducing in them a spirit of prayer, especially in two of the deacons, who were particularly importunate that God would visit us in mercy, and render the Word of His grace effectual amongst us for the conversion of sinners." *

What is especially to be noticed in this experience is its relation to the Church of God. When the ice was melted from his own soul, then he began to plead for all the saints and all the ministers. And, as afterwards appears, at the same time that the Spirit fell on him it was falling on his brethren in distant places. So it is always. God never makes half a providence any more than man makes half a pair of shears. If He fits a preacher to declare His Word, He fits a hearer to receive that Word ; if He moves one soul to cry, "What must I do?" He has

* "Life and Sermons," p. 28.

always moved some other servant of His to direct him what to do. Let us ponder the story of Paul and Ananias, of Peter and Cornelius, of Philip and the eunuch, if we would observe the mystery of the Spirit—His twofold ministry, to preacher and to hearer, to counsellor and to inquirer. And noting this, we shall understand the intimate relationship between the season of renewal in the heart of the individual believer and the time of reviving in the Church. If two harp-strings are in perfect tune, you cannot smite the one without causing the other to vibrate; and if one Christian is touched and agitated by the Spirit of God, think it not strange that all who are like-minded in the Church are moved by the same divine impulse. Not for ourselves, and that we may enjoy the holy luxury of communion with God, are we to seek for the times of refreshing. If so, doubtless we shall fail of them, for even spiritual blessings we may ask and receive not, if we only ask that we may consume them upon ourselves.

No biography to which we have been introduced seems to us more instructive on this point than that of David Brainerd. From time to time he sought and obtained the holiest intimacies with God, yet never for himself. Trace, line by line, the following remarkable passage from his diary:—

"APRIL 19, 1742.—I set apart this day for fasting and prayer to God for His grace; especially to prepare me for the work of the ministry, to give me divine aid and direction in my preparations for that great work, and in His own time to send me into His harvest. Accordingly, in the morning I endeavoured to plead for the Divine Presence for the day, and not without some life. In the forenoon I felt the power of intercession for precious, immortal souls, for the advancement of the kingdom of my dear Lord and Saviour in the world, and, withal, a most sweet resignation and even consolation and joy in the thought of suffering hardships, distresses, and even death itself, in the promotion of it; and had special enlargement in pleading for the enlightening and conversion of the poor heathen. In the afternoon God was with me of a truth. Oh, it was blessed company indeed! God enabled me so to agonize in prayer that I was quite wet with sweat, though in the shade and the cool wind. *My soul was drawn out very much for the world; I grasped for multitudes of souls. I think I had more enlargement for sinners than for the children of God, though I felt as if I could spend my life in cries for both.* I had great enjoyment in communion with my dear Saviour. I think I never in my life felt such an entire weanedness from this world, and so much resigned to God in everything. Oh that I may always live to and upon my blessed God! Amen, amen." *

Here, certainly, is something very high and remote from ordinary experience—this praying one's self into fellowship with Christ's sufferings, and into partnership with His garden sweat. But we are writing now for those who wish to know concerning the highest attainments. Yet what we are especially emphasizing is the relation of these extraordinary experiences to the furtherance of the gospel and the salvation of souls.

* "Memoir," p. 46.

He who in thus interceding grasped not for some ecstatic vision or revelation of God, but "for multitudes of souls," gained what he sought; for marvellous power attended his preaching. There were days in which the Spirit of God fell upon those stolid, hard-hearted Indians with such demonstration that scores of them bowed before the preacher like grass before the mower's scythe ; so that even the ambassador himself was astonished, and ex- claimed, "And there was no day like that before it or after it."

Brainerd had many seasons of this uncommon renewing of his spiritual life through prayer and fasting ; and in summing them up, President Edwards records this noteworthy conclusion : " Among all the many days he spent in secret prayer and fasting, of which he gives an account in his diary, *there is scarcely an instance of one which was not either attended or soon followed with apparent success, and a remarkable blessing in special influences and consolations of God's Spirit, and very often before the day was ended."* And we may add yet more. The record of these fastings and prayers of Brainerd, and of the power of God which followed, written only for himself, but wisely published by Edwards after his death, has brought rich blessing to the world. William Carey read it on his shoemaker's bench, and asked, " If God can do such things among the Indians of America, why not among the pagans of India ? " Henry Martyn, the thoughtful student in Cambridge, England, read it, and was moved by it to consecrate his life to missionary service in the East. Edward Payson pondered it, and when twenty-two years of age wrote in his diary : " In reading Mr. Brainerd's life, I seemed to feel a most earnest desire after some portion of his spirit." Considering the vast results which have followed the labours of these servants of God, who shall say that Brainerd has not wrought even more since his death than in his life ?* And who, looking at the great sum total, can question whether or not it is profitable for one to wait upon the Lord with prayer, and fasting, and intercession, for the renewal of his spiritual strength ? O Holy Spirit, quicken us by Thy mighty power, so that we may " put off concerning the former conversation the old man, which is corrupt according to the deceitful lusts ; and be renewed in the spirit of our mind ; *and that we may put on the new man, which after God is created in righteousness and true holiness.*"

---

* " JUNE 27, 1832.—Life of David Brainerd. Most wonderful man ! What conflicts, what depressions, desertions, strength, advancement, victories within thy torn bosom ! I cannot express what I think when I think of thee. To-night more set on missionary enterprise than ever."—*McCheyne's Journal.*

CONVERSION AND CONSECRATION.

" I MUST say that I never have had so close and satis
factory a view of the gospel salvation, as when I have beei
led to contemplate it in the light of a simple offer on th
one side, and a simple acceptance on the other."—*Thoma.
Chalmers.*

" FULL consecration may in one sense be the act of :
moment, and in another the work of a lifetime. It must b
complete to be real, and yet, if real, it is always incomplete
a point of rest, and yet a perpetual progression. Suppos
you make over a piece of ground to another person. Fror
the moment of giving the title-deed, it is no longer you
possession ; it is entirely his. But his practical occupatio
of it may not appear all at once. There may be waste lan
which he will take into cultivation only by degrees. . . . Jus
so it is with our lives. The transaction of, so to speak
making them over to God is definite and complete. But the
begins the practical development of consecration."—*France
Ridley Havergal.*

III.

CONVERSION AND CONSECRATION.

THESE two facts in our spiritual history seem to us to be often strangely confounded. We make a radical distinction between them. In conversion we receive; in consecration we give; in the one we accept eternal life from God; in the other we offer up ourselves in self-surrender to God; in the one we appropriate the work of Christ done for us, in the other we fulfil the work of the Spirit in us. Inquirers are not infrequently counselled to give their hearts to Christ, or to consecrate themselves to the Lord. We would not be over-critical with what is well meant; but really this is not the Gospel. The good news of grace is that God hath given to us eternal life and redemption through His Son, and that in order to be saved the sinner has nought to do but to accept it. Indeed, why should one be asked to give, when he has nothing acceptable to bring?

" It is more blessed to give than to receive "; and the Lord, who is alone worthy, takes this highest beatitude for Himself, and puts the whole

race of unrenewed sinners into the position of
helpless and dependent receivers.*

"For God so loved the world, that *He gave* His only-begotten Son " (John iii. 16).	"*As many as received* Him, to them gave He power to become the sons of God " (John i. 12).
"*The gift* of God is eternal life" (Rom. vi. 23).	"Whosoever will, *let him take* the water of life freely " (Rev. xxii. 17).
"Christ also loved the church, and *gave Himself* for it " (Eph. v. 25).	"As ye have therefore *received Christ Jesus the Lord*" (Col. ii. 6).

But having received the gift of God and been
made a partaker of His converting grace, and then
and therefore the divine obligation for service begins
to press upon us. The Lord becomes an asker
as soon as we have become recipients "*As ye
have therefore received Christ Jesus the Lord, so
walk ye in Him ;*" † let consecration crown conversion, let self-devotement to Christ answer to His
self-devotement for you. Has the reader noticed
the significant " *therefore* " in that earnest plea for consecration with which the twelfth of Romans opens ?
Just previously the question has been asked, " Or

---

* "The gospel of the grace of God does not consist in pressing
the duty defined by the words ' *Give your heart to Christ*,' although
that is often unwisely urged upon inquirers after salvation as though
it were the gospel. The true gospel is, ' *Accept the free gift of salvation from wrath and sin by receiving Jesus Himself and all the
benefits He purchased with His blood.*"—WILLIAM REID : *Blood of
Jesus*, p. 22.

† Col. ii. 6.

who hath first given to Him, and it shall be recompensed unto him again?" Had we first rendered something to God, we might look for a return. But, on the contrary, we have received everything from Him—"*for of Him and through Him* and to Him are all things." And this is the reason why we should render to Him all that we have. " I beseech you, *therefore*, brethren, by the mercies of God, that ye present your bodies a living sacrifice, holy, acceptable unto God, which is your reasonable service."

One love demands another. If God has shown His love to us by giving His Son to die as a sacrifice for our sins, let us show our love by giving ourselves to live in daily sacrifice for Him. " By giving ourselves," we say. Self-sacrifice may be scanted in two ways. We may give our possessions, instead of giving ourselves ; or we may give ourselves to God's service instead of to God Himself. In either case our sacrifice is lame and our consecration lacking. There must be self-surrender to Him who surrendered Himself for us, before Christ can be "all, and in all." Have we not found persons giving their money to charity, under the idea that their gift would in some way sanctify the giver and make him acceptable to the Lord ? But God requires our persons before He asks our purses. We are to " present our bodies" unto Him, and that will carry our possessions. For the body is "the temple of the Holy Ghost," and Jesus tells us that it is the

2

temple that sanctifies the gold, and not the gold that sanctifies the temple.   The devotement of self, therefore, must go before devotement of property and possessions.   This is the divine order which the Apostle so thankfully recognizes in acknowledging the gifts of the Macedonian Christians.   For making mention of the riches of their liberality, he adds, " And this they did, not as we expected, but *first gave their own selves to the Lord, and unto us by the will of God.*" *   And for this cause he declares that he ministered the gospel of God to the Gentiles, that being renewed by the Spirit, they might be fitted to give in the Spirit, " that the offering up of the Gentiles might be acceptable, being sanctified by the Holy Ghost." †   And the opposite idea is equally true—that we must devote ourselves *to the Lord*, not merely to some work for the Lord, which may absorb in itself the interest and zeal which should be bestowed on His divine person.

Now nothing is clearer than the fact that a Christian gets power from God, just in proportion to the entireness of his self-surrender to God.   If we ask how this is, the answer is easy.   It is not that God keeps a strictly debt and credit account with the Christian, giving so much grace for so much sacrifice, so much power for so much humility.   It is by the action of a necessary law that it comes to pass.   We know that, in the human body, the privation of any one of the senses only intensifies

---

* 2 Cor. viii. 5.   † Rom. xv. 16.

the power of those which remain. If, for example, the sight be lost, the touch and taste become thereby much more acute. Exactly so it is between the three factors of our human being—body, soul, and spirit ; whatever either one surrenders is carried over to the credit of the others, and inures to their strength. That is why fasting helps communion—the carnal appetites being denied that the spiritua. appetites may be awakened to a more hungry craving. Hence the significance of the plea that we present our *bodies* a living sacrifice. We should have said " bodies and spirits," and many so enlarge the exhortation. But no ! Let the body be surrendered up for the enrichment of the soul, fleshly desires repressed, that spiritual desires may be enlarged—the carnal man, in a word, sacrificed to the spiritual.

We have seen this significant device on an ancient seal—the effigy of a burning candle, and underneath it the superscription, " *I give light by being myself consumed.*" This is the true symbol of Christian devotedness—giving out light by giving up our lives to Him who loved us—the zeal of God's house consuming us while we furnish divine illumination to the world.

And this leads us to urge what we believe to be all-important to this whole subject—that we should make our consecration a definite, final, and irrevocable event in our spiritual history. It is not enough for us to hear one say that he believes in Jesus Christ ;

we want a decisive and confessed act of acceptance. And likewise we are not satisfied to urge upon our readers a consecrated life merely ; we wish to insist on the value and power of a solemn and definite and overshadowing act of consecration. Let it be made with the utmost deliberation, and after the most prayerful self-examination ; let the seal of God's acceptance of it be most carefully sought ; let it be final, in the sense of being irrevocable, but initiatory in the sense of being introductory to a new life—a life that belongs, henceforth, utterly to God, to be lived where He would have it lived, to be employed as He would have it employed, to be finished when He would have it finished. Oh, who is sufficient for such an engagement ! But many have made it, and we find in them a living demonstration of its value.

In the spiritual history of George Whitfield we have a striking example of such definite and wholehearted consecration. With the Wesleys in the " Holy Club " of Oxford, he had sought with prolonged prayer and self-mortification for a deeper work of the Spirit in his heart. Whole days he had spent in wrestling with God for the blessing. He found what he sought, and, at his ordination, was made ready to give himself unreservedly to God. He thus speaks of this experience :—

" When the Bishop laid his hands upon my head, if my evil heart doth not deceive me, *I offered up my whole spirit, soul, and body, to the service of God's sanctuary.* Let come what will, life or death, depth or height, I shall henceforth live like one who this day, in the presence of men and angels, took the holy sacrament upon the profession of being inwardly moved by the Holy Ghost to take upon me that ministration in the Church." "*I can call heaven and earth to witness that, when the Bishop laid his hand upon me, I gave myself up, to be a martyr for Him who hung upon the cross for me.* Known unto Him are all future events and contingencies. I have thrown myself blindfolded, and I trust without reserve, into His almighty hands." *

Such was his vow of self-devotion to God, and it must be acknowledged that his whole subsequent life attested its sincerity. And in what life, we may ask, has the power of consecration been more signally displayed ? We speak not merely of his seraphic eloquence, but of the immediate saving results of his preaching. We judge that other preachers have produced as powerful impression upon congregations—Bossuet, Robert Hall, Chalmers, and many more. But that lightning-like penetration of the spoken word which rives men's hearts, and lays bare their sins, and brings out the tears of penitence—here is the test of power. And from the very first sermon of Whitfield, when fifteen were driven to an agony of conviction, to the last, this was the uniform 'result of his ministry. John Newton records of him that in a single week he received no less than a thousand letters from those distressed in conscience under his preaching. Surely

---

* Stevens' "History of Methodism," Vol. I., p. 105.

this was not the fruit of his " graceful oratory," which Franklin and Chesterfield so much admired ; but of that power from on high which is promised to those who are ready to tarry in Jerusalem until they be endued with it. How significant the Apostle's description of effective preaching ! " For our gospel came not unto you in word only, *but also in power and in the Holy Ghost, and in much assurance."* *

Words, kindled and glowing with the fire of intellectual excitement, can rouse and thrill and overpower, till the effect seems something quite supernatural. But intellect and the Holy Spirit must not be confounded. The highest reach of genius comes far short of the lowest degree of inspiration. To electrify a hearer is one thing ; to bring a hearer prostrate at the feet of Jesus is quite another. The one effect is " in word only " ; the other is " in power and in the Holy Ghost." And the latter result we have often seen accomplished through the plainest speech, and by the humblest instruments. But how subtle and elusive is the " power " ! He who desires it for the sake of being great, can no more have it than Simon Magus could buy it with money. How many a servant of God has quenched the Spirit in his inordinate desire to shine ; how often has the soul-winner gone out of the pulpit because the orator has come in and filled the entire foreground with himself. So then the

---

* I Thess. i. 5.

rhetorician cannot teach us the secret. He can help us in word only. The consecration, by which we put ourselves utterly into the hands of God, to be subject to His will and to be swayed by His Spirit, is the only true pathway to power.

Of course as there are diversities of gifts from the same Spirit, so the manifestations of spiritual energy will be widely various.

We will select an example which stands in total contrast from that just considered. Stephen Grellet, the saintly Quaker, was endued with extraordinary power as a witness for Christ. " Over two hemispheres he bore a testimony adapted, with marvellous wisdom, alike to dwellers in palaces and in slaves' huts ; to the inmates of ecclesiastical mansions and common jails, and yet none the less suited to the periodic meetings of Friends, and to large assemblies of Roman Catholics and Protestants, in Europe and America."* His was pre-eminently a ministry of love. The word in the mouth of Whitfield was a sharp two-edged sword, piercing and wounding unto life eternal. From the lips of Grellet that word distilled like the dew, even " as the dew of Hermon that descended upon the mountains of Zion ; for there the Lord commanded the blessing, even life for evermore."

If we ask whence this strange enchantment which he threw over human hearts so that they opened to his words irresistibly, in spite of prejudice and stern

---

* " Life of Stephen Grellet," by William Guest, p. 3.

tradition, the answer is easily found. It was the
love of Christ acting divinely through one who had
given himself up to be led of God, and who, as he
wrote on the last page of his journal, had learned
the habit of " *keeping a single eye to the putting forth
of the Divine Spirit.*" This good man had had his
Pentecost,—blessed and never to be forgotten, from
which he dated a new enduement of power. Referring to the time and place of this transaction he
says :—

"There the Lord was pleased, in an humbling and
memorable manner, to visit me again and to comfort me.
I had gone into the woods, which are there mostly of very
lofty and large pines, and my mind being inwardly retired
before the Lord, He was pleased so to reveal His love to
me, through His blessed Son, my Saviour, that many fears
and doubts were at that ·time removed, my soul's wounds
were healed, my mourning was turned into joy.   He
clothed me with the garment of praise, instead of the spirit
of heaviness, and He strengthened me *to offer up myself
again freely to Him and to His service for my whole life.*
Walk, O my soul, in that path which thy blessed Master
has trodden before thee and has consecrated for thee.   Be
willing also to die to thyself, that thou mayest live through
faith in Him."

Here is a life which constituted a kind of living
exegesis of that text, " speaking the truth in love."
And, accustomed as we are to measure power by
outward demonstration, it furnishes a most instructive lesson for us. Two chemical elements which
are very mild and innocuous in themselves, often

have prodigious energy when combined. So it is of
love and truth. Those who preach love alone are
often the weakest and most ineffective witnesses for
Christ. Those who preach the truth alone, not
infrequently demonstrate the feebleness of a soulless
orthodoxy. But the truth in love is vital, penetrating, and has the dynamic force which we seek. See
how Paul, the apostle of truth, and John, the apostle
of love, match and supplement each other on this
point. " *Speaking the truth in love,*" writes the one.
" Unto the well-beloved Gaius, *whom I love in the
truth,*" writes the other. Love furnishing the atmosphere of truth, the medium through which it shines,
and by which it is transmitted ; and truth lending
its gravity and restraint to love, and so preventing it
from flying off into a reckless and indiscriminate
toleration,—this is the combination which gives true
power. "Grace is poured into thy lips ; *therefore
God hath blessed thee for ever.*" Grace that wings the
gentle speech ; grace that imparts the heavenly
unction ; grace that is invested with " the irresist-
ible might of weakness,"—this is the true secret
of divine efficiency,—and yet only half the secret.
" Grace *and truth* came by Jesus Christ. Oh for
a conformity to Christ and a non-conformity to the
world, that shall enable us to grasp both these gifts !
Then the highway of power will be open before us,
and we may realize the beautiful ideal of the faithful
witness : " He had eyes lifted up to heaven, the
best of books was in his hand, *the law of truth was*

written upon his lips, the world was behind his back. He stood as if he pleaded with men ; and a crown of glory did hang over his head." *

Let it not be presumed, however, that the way of consecration is a way exempt from sacrifices and perils. One who moves in this direction is certain to encounter the adversary at every step. The moment the believer makes any determined advance toward holiness, that moment the evil one moves up his picket line for desperate resistance. Pastor Blumhardt—who in this generation has wrought such conquests in prayer and faith—lays special emphasis on this point, telling us that " he who is ignorant of the wiles and artifices of the enemy, only beats the air, and the devil is not afraid of him." Let the reader study the life of this remarkable man, if he would learn what possibilities of spiritual power are still open to us. Amid the freezing rationalism of Tübingen University, here was one young heart which kept itself kindled with the fire of Pentecost, and by surrendering itself up n daily co nsecration, was preparing to give the world a living demonstration of the things which the learned men of that university had set themselves to deny. We see him raising the sick by his prayers, casting out devils, and bringing whole communities to the foot of the cross in penitence. But Satan was always at his right hand to resist him. " In interesting my-self in behalf of one possessed," he writes, " I became

* Bunyan.

involved in such a fearful conflict with the powers of darkness, as is not possible for me to describe." Underscore this passage, oh reader. It has a broad significance. When something extraordinary is to be done for Christ, hell from beneath will be moved to resist it. The marks of Martin Luther's inkstand on Wartburg castle are not the traces of a pitiable superstition. Here is a man who is to shake all Europe with a new revival, and where on earth or under the earth is Satan so likely to mass his forces as in this monk's cell? Brother Martin is not throwing his ink-horn at a phantom when he hurls it at the devil. It is very necessary to touch on this point, because every aspirant after holiness is certain to be assailed with peculiar conflicts and temptations; and it is natural to regard these as indications that dangerous ground has been entered upon, when they are often only evidences that we are entering upon higher ground.

That gifted woman in whom inspiration and aspiration were so beautifully blended, Frances Ridley Havergal, makes a cheering comment on a familiar text of Scripture—" Behold, I give unto you power to tread on serpents and scorpions, and over all the power of the enemy." Why this is grand," she writes, "*power over all the power* of the enemy. Just where he is strongest, there they shall prevail. Not over his weak points and places, but over the very centre of his power; not over his power here and there, or now and then, but over *all* his power.

And Jesus said it. Isn't it enough to go into battle with ? " *

She was encouraging her own heart when she wrote these words. What a lofty path of spirituality she traversed ! Has the reader of her biography marked the open secret of her consecrated career ? It is found in the same experience, of which we have spoken elsewhere, of definite, whole-souled devotement to God. This is the record of it, which she has left behind :—

"It was on Advent Sunday, December, 1873, that I first saw clearly the blessedness of true consecration. I saw it as a flash of electric light; and what you see, you can never unsee. *There must be full surrender before there can be full blessedness. God admits you by the one into the other.* He Himself showed me this most clearly. You know how singularly I have been withheld from attending conventions and conferences; man's teaching has consequently but little to do with it. First I was shown that the blood of Jesus Christ, His Son, cleanseth from all sin ; and then it was made plain to me that He who had thus cleansed me, had power to keep me clean; *so I utterly yielded myself to Him and utterly trusted Him to keep me.*"

In literature and in life, she served her generation with rare effectiveness. Her works are suffused with a beautiful glow of spiritual health ; and in reading her books of sacred poetry and devotion, honoured with an almost unprecedented circulation, we wonder if any one in our day has spoken more directly to

---

* "Memorials of Frances R. Havergal," p. 10.

he heart of man, and more directly from the heart
)f God. And thus the lesson is pressed upon us
mew of the power of a sanctified life.

In treating thus of special acts of consecration,
ve would interpose a caution against written cove-
1ants with God. To yield ourselves up to Him in
ull self-surrender is one thing ; to bind ourselves to
lo and to suffer certain things for Him is quite
mother. The divine nature within us may be
:trong enough to perform such vows, but human
1ature is insolvent, and all its promises are but a
)ankrupt's bond. And this human nature is still a
)artner in the firm that makes the contract, just as
)ur Lord so solemnly declared in the face of His
lisciples' failure and desertion. " The spirit indeed
s willing, *but the flesh is weak."* Dr. Doddridge
·ecommended a written compact with the Lord.
' Set your hand and seal to it, that on such a day of
;uch a month and year, and at such a place, on full
:onsideration and serious reflection, you came to the
1appy resolution, that whatever others might do,
/ou would serve the Lord." The excellent Samuel
Pearce of Birmingham followed this advice in his
:arly Christian life. He wrote his solemn league
md covenant with God, and to make it the more
)inding he opened a vein in his arm and signed it
vith his own blood. But when in a little while he
ound how utterly he had broken this sacred
:ngagement, he was plunged into despair, and only
ound release when he tore up the document and

scattered it to the winds, and cast himself hence
forth entirely upon the "blood of the everlasting
covenant." *

We do not say that such a method can never be
of use. It may in some instances. John Frederick
Oberlin, the devoted and apostolic pastor, seems to
have found it so. He certainly furnishes another
striking illustration of the influence of definite and
entire consecration. Let one read of the astonish-
ing change effected through his ministry in the
morals and condition of his little flock in Waldbach
amid the wilds of Northern France; or let one
ponder the exquisite story of the orphan girl, Louise
Schepler, so impressed by the holiness and self-
denial of this good pastor's life, that she begged the
privilege of serving him without wages or reward,
so long as she should live. The clue to his remarkable power may doubtless be found in a document
which was left among his papers. It is long, but
we give a paragraph which contains its pith and
substance :—

"In the name of the Lord of hosts, I this day renounce
all former lords that have had dominion over me, the joys
of the world in which I have too much delighted, and all

---

* John Howe, in his discourse on Self-dedication, tells of a devout
French nobleman who made a quit-claim deed of himself to God, and
signed the document with his own blood—" whose affection I commend,"
he adds, "more than his expression of it." And well he might. When
God takes security He wants a good name and a trustworthy signature.
We are only safe when we present "the name above every name," and
trust alone in "the blood of the New Testament."

carnal desires. I renounce all perishable things in order
that God may constitute my All. *I consecrate to Thee all
that I am, and all that I have; the faculties of my mind, the
members of my body, my fortune, and my time.* Grant me
grace, O Father of mercies, to employ all to Thy glory, and
in obedience to Thy commands. For ardently and humbly
I desire to be Thine through the endless ages of eternity.
Should Thou be pleased to make me in this life the instrument in leading others to Thee, give me strength and
courage openly to declare Thy Name. And enable me, not
only to devote myself to Thy service, but to persuade my
brethren to dedicate themselves to it also."[*]

    Strasbourg, 1st January, 1760.
  Renewed at Waldbach, 1st January, 1770.

We have given quite enough in these examples
to exhibit the intimate and certain relation of personal consecration to spiritual power. But in all
that we have said, we have assumed that the Holy
Spirit is the Sanctifier and Sealer of this consecration. Our Lord Jesus Christ here, as in all things,
is our Pattern and Exemplar. " For their sakes I
sanctify Myself, that they also might be sanctified
through the truth." [†] Exemplar, we said. He is
more than this—He is our life. It is His divine
nature working in us which can alone effect this
great transaction. He acted in and through the
Holy Ghost in His self-devotement—" Who *through
the Eternal Spirit* offered Himself without spot unto
God." [‡] How much more must we rely upon that
divine inworking ! We need the Spirit by whom to

---

  [*] "Life of Oberlin," p. 26.   [†] John xvii. 19.   [‡] Heb. ix. 14.

seek the Spirit, Christ's consecration by which to consecrate ourselves, God's supreme gift, the Comforter, by whom to give ourselves to God.   Oh, Holy Spirit, who dost make our bodies Thy habitation, consecrate that in which Thou dost dwell, that it may be " a vessel unto honour, sanctified and meet for the Master's use, and prepared unto every good work."

SALVATION AND SEALING.

"FAITH saves us; but how?—by making us aware of Christ, who saves. Faith does not *make* things what they are, but *shows* us them as they are in Christ. Certain systems lay a pressure upon the subjective side greater than the spirit of man is at all times able to bear; working out all things from the depths of individual consciousness as if truths were not there at all until they are *manifestly* there for us. Happy for us if Christ can look there and find His own image reflected, however faintly; but *we* must look at Him, at the sun in the heavens, not at the sun in the brook, its broken and ever varying reflection."—*Dora Greenwell.*

"IF we can learn aright how Christ was sealed, we shall learn how we are sealed. The sealing of Christ by the Father was the communication of the Holy Ghost in all His fullness to Him, authorizing Him unto and acting His Divine power in all the acts and duties of His office, so as to evidence the presence of God unto Him and appropriation of Him. So in God's sealing of believers He owns them and gives them His Holy Spirit to fit them for their relations, to enable them unto their duties, to act their new principles, and every way to discharge the work they are called to do. He gives them the Spirit of power, of love, and of a sound mind. And hereby does God seal them."—*John Owen.*

IV.

SALVATION AND SEALING.

FAITH in the promise and in the person of Jesus Christ is that which secures salvation to us ; the enduement of the Holy Spirit is that which gives us power in labouring for the salvation of others. The word on which we rest for the one blessing is, "Verily, verily, I say unto you, He that believeth on Me hath everlasting life" ; the word on which we rest for the other blessing is, "Ye shall receive power after that the Holy Ghost is come upon you." And we find in Scripture that there are two seals for attesting these two promises :—

"He that hath received His testimony *hath set to his seal that God is true*" (John iii. 33).

"After that ye believed *ye were sealed with the Holy Spirit of Promise*" (Eph. i. 13).

Very simple and beautiful is the way of faith as described in the first of these texts. To believe what God says concerning His Son is the first requirement for obeying the Gospel. Faith simply believes what God has declared, and accepts what He has done for us through the redemption of His Son. And here is the sharp distinction between

him that believeth and him that believeth not.
God has borne witness to His Son that He is the
Christ. "Who is a liar but he that denieth that
Jesus is the Christ?" asks John; but "Whosoever
believeth that Jesus is the Christ is born of God," *
says the same Apostle. Such is the great gulf
between faith and unbelief. Again, God has declared that we have life in His Son, and in Him alone.
"And this is the record, that God hath given to us
eternal life, and this life is in His Son." † But says
the Scripture once more, "He that believeth not
God *hath made Him a liar* because he believeth not
the record that God gave of His Son"; while on
the contrary, "he that receiveth His testimony hath
set to his seal *that God is true.*"

Now we cannot emphasize the fact too strongly,
that it is faith in the Son of God and faith only
by which we are saved. Feeling may act very
powerfully in connection with the Spirit's work in us,
but it is faith alone that can appropriate Christ's
work for us. And in no way can we so honour
God as by taking His promise, "He that believeth
on the Son hath life," and stamping it with the
signet of our faith—"*That is true.*" Not because
we have proved it or felt it, but because God has
said it, is our assurance. "Said I not unto thee
that *if thou wouldest believe*, thou shouldst see the
glory of God?" asks Jesus. Our order would have
been, let me first see and then I will believe. But

---

* 1 John v. 1.   † 1 John v. 10, 11.

trust is never so simple and genuine as when it is
blind, and has nothing to rest on but the bare word
of God.   Faith and reason are like the two compart-
ments of an hour-glass ; the one can only be full
when the other is empty.   That is to say, faith
is at its best when it has nothing of proof or reason
to rest upon, but grounds its assurance absolutely in
the testimony of the Lord ; and it is at its least
when it believes only because of clear demonstration.
Whatever of evidence or emotion therefore comes in
as proof, detracts just so much from faith's simplicity, and from our full share in the benediction,
" Blessed are they that *have not seen* and yet have
believed." *   Again and again the Scriptures declare that he that believeth on the Son *hath*
eternal life—hath it, that is, in germ and embryo,
as one has the harvest who has the seed from which
it springs.   The words of Scripture are called
indeed " the incorruptible seed."   To receive and
credit the word of God concerning His Son is therefore to receive life or regeneration.   " Being born
again not of corruptible seed but of incorruptible,
by the Word of God, which liveth and abideth for
ever." †

Thus in the beginning it was those that " gladly
received the word " that were baptized and added
to the Church.   All this puts weighty emphasis on
the duty we have been urging, of sealing God's
promises with our hearty and confident amen.   And

* John xx. 29.   † 1 Peter i. 23.

we would commend a faith that even seems auda-
cious, like that of the sturdy Covenanter, Robert
Bruce, who requested, as he was dying, that his finger
might be placed on one of God's strong promises, as
though to challenge the Judge of all with it as he
should enter His presence.* As we stand face to
face with the Word we cannot be too bold.

There is again another sealing which is mentioned
in the Scriptures, and which supplements this as a
divine testimony to the fact of acceptance. "*After
that ye believed ye were sealed* with the Holy Spirit
of promise,"† says Paul, writing to the Ephesians.
There are many allusions in Scripture to this transaction, and the general tenor of these references indi-
cates that it is a special enduement of the Spirit
subsequent to that regeneration of the Spirit which
takes place when one believes. Such is the inference
in the Epistle to the Corinthians, where the Apostle,
addressing those who have been established in the
promises of God, adds, "*Who hath also sealed us*, and
given the earnest of the Spirit in our hearts." ‡ As
our faith authenticates the Lord's promise by setting
to it our yea and amen, the Holy Spirit now
authenticates us as the sons of God by giving to us

* A sublime instance of this boldness of faith is given by Dr. John
Brown, in his *Horæ Subsecivæ*, of a Scotch woman who was asked on
her death-bed, "What would you say if God, after all He has done,
should let you drop into hell?" She replied, "E'en as He likes ; but
if He does He'll lose mair than I'll do."

† Eph. i. 13, "In whom having also believed ye were sealed with
the Holy Spirit of Promise" (Revised Version).

‡ 2 Cor. i. 22.

the first-fruits of our inheritance, in the joy and assurance and guidance and strength of the indwelling Comforter. On this ground rests the solemn appeal in the Epistle to the Ephesians—"Grieve not the Spirit of God *in whom ye were sealed* unto the day of redemption."*

While there is much that is mysterious and difficult to apprehend in this subject, we believe that we can get more light concerning it from the example and experience of Jesus Christ than anywhere else, since He is the pattern for His brethren in all things. Jesus says, referring to Himself, "*For Him hath God the Father sealed.*" † This evidently refers to what took place at His baptism. Let us go to the banks of the Jordan and witness the divine transaction and that which follows it. As He comes forth from the water we see "*the Spirit of God descending like a dove and lighting upon Him;* a voice is heard from heaven saying, "*This is My beloved Son,* in whom I am well pleased"; Jesus "being *full of the Holy Ghost,* returned from the Jordan"; He is "*led by the Spirit* into the wilderness"; He afterwards returns "*in the power of the Spirit*"; and going into the synagogue, He applies to Himself the words of the prophet, "The Spirit of the Lord is upon Me because *He hath anointed Me to preach the gospel to the poor.*" ‡

This was our Lord's enduement or sealing by the Holy Ghost in preparation for His public service.

---

* Eph. iv. 30.　　† John vi. 27.　　‡ Luke iv. 1-20.

And what an impressive lesson it is for us, that,
though He was the divine Son of God, yet He henceforth did all things in dependence upon the Spirit ;
from the beginning of His ministry, when He said,
"*I by the Spirit of God* cast out devils," to the end
when " *through the Eternal Spirit* He offered up Himself without spot unto God." Now mark how every
feature of the Lord's sealing is reproduced in that of
His disciples, after the Holy Ghost has come upon
them. They also have the assurance of sonship ;
" the Spirit Himself beareth witness with our spirits
that we are the children of God." * They have the
same divine guidance, " for as many as *are led by the
Spirit of God*, they are the sons of God." † They
are indwelt by the same Spirit ; " and they were all
filled with the Holy Ghost." ‡ They are endued
with the same energy ; "*ye shall receive power* after
that the Holy Ghost is come upon you." They
have the same divine unction ; " *the anointing which
ye have received abideth on you.*"

Here certainly is one seal for both Master and
disciple, since all the lines and features of the two
impressions exactly correspond. In the case of
Jesus Christ, this transaction was a distinct and
divine enduement for His public ministry. Is it so
with His followers ? Certainly it was with the first
disciples. The same event happened to the body
of believers on the day of Pentecost which befell the

* Rom. viii. 16.   † Rom. viii. 14.
‡ Acts ii. 4 ; i. 8.   1 John ii. 27.

Lord at the Jordan. Both alike were baptized with the Holy Ghost. " Is the day of Pentecost, then, to be perpetually repeated ? " it will be asked. To which we answer, " No ! and yes ! " As the inauguration of the Spirit's ministry in the Church it cannot be repeated. On that day the Holy Ghost in His abiding personal presence came into the Church to guide and order and inspire it henceforth throughout this dispensation. As Christmas was the incarnation of the Second Person of the Trinity, when the Word was made flesh and tabernacled among us, so Pentecost was a kind of incarnation of the Third Person when the Holy Spirit came to dwell in the body of believers, so that each Christian is now " the temple of the Holy Ghost," and the whole Church is " the habitation of God through the Spirit."

Since this wonderful event has come to pass, the Holy Spirit's home and place of ministry is here on earth, just as truly as Jesus Christ's present habitation and seat of intercession is in heaven at God's right hand. Therefore we need not pray for the Comforter to be sent down, for He is here as truly as Christ was here in the days of His humiliation. But while this is true, we are to remember that the presence of the Spirit is one thing, and the power and fullness of the Spirit another. When Jesus sent forth the seventy on their ministry of grace He said, " *Behold, I give unto you power,*" * and then

* Luke x. 19.

invested them with His own divine prerogatives of
preaching, and healing, and casting out demons.
So the Spirit who is now present in the Church gives
power for service to those who seek it.   In this
sense the experience of Pentecost can be repeated.
It is still our privilege to pray for the baptism of
the Spirit, and to tarry in supplication until we be
"endued with power from on high."   And a careful reading of the Acts of the Apostles would seem
to indicate that this experience is something quite
distinct from regeneration, being no less than an
investment of the believer with a special divine
energy and efficiency for carrying on God's work.*
"Did   ye   receive   the   Holy   Ghost   when   ye
believed?"† asks   Paul   of   certain   disciples   at
Ephesus.   Believers   and   disciples   they   certainly
were, but this did not carry the certainty with
it that they had received the power of the Spirit.
On the contrary, they lacked this until by the laying
on of the apostles' hands "the Holy Ghost came
upon them"; then they "spoke with tongues and

---

* "God's sealing of believers is His gracious communication of the
Holy Ghost unto them, *so to act by divine power in them as to enable
them unto all the duties of their holy calling*, evidencing them to be
accepted with Him both to themselves and others, and asserting their
preservation unto eternal salvation.   The effects of this sealing are,
gracious operations of the Spirit in and upon believers, but the sealing
itself is the communication of the Spirit unto them.   For it is not said
that the Holy Ghost seals us, but that we are sealed with Him.   He
is God's seal unto us. . . . Where God sets this seal, such effects
will be produced as shall fall under the observation of the world."—
John Owen (1616-1683).

† Acts xix. 2 (Revised Version).

prophesied." After the day of Pentecost we hear Peter urging his hearers, by obeying the gospel, to seek for "the gift of the Holy Ghost," adding, "for the promise is unto you and to your children, and to all that are afar off, even as many as the Lord our God shall call." So that like the upper-room disciples we can come pleading an explicit promise when we ask for the fullness, and power, and indwelling of the Comforter.

Have we noticed how almost every great conquest of preaching or working recorded in the Acts is introduced by the words, " *and being filled with the Holy Ghost*," * he did thus ? In this record of the early Church's history we have the autobiography of the Holy Ghost, if we may say so ; or rather the opening chapter of such an autobiography. It is the acts of the Spirit, as He moves and empowers men, of which we are here reading. Have there been no subsequent chapters of this book unfolding in these later times ? Let the lives of some modern saints as they shall pass before us answer this question. Let us look at their closet exercises, and at their field conquests, and ask if it does not seem that we have in these latter-day Christians a fac-simile of the sealing and wonder working of the first disciples.

Now sealing we hold to be the divine side of consecration—God's token of approval and acceptance of our self-surrender to Him. When the soul offers itself as the soft and plastic wax He can stamp

* Acts iv. 8, 13, 19. Eph. v. 18.

it with His signet-ring, marking it thus as His own
peculiar property, and setting it apart for His own
peculiar use until the day of redemption. Often the
sealing is effected without observation or recognition
on the part of its subject. Its *traits* are visible,
—assurance of adoption, power in testimony, the
joy of the Holy Ghost, and the blessed sense of
belonging entirely to the Lord. These constitute
the signature of the Spirit's work upon the heart.
But the operation itself may have been quite silent
and unobserved. On the other hand, in scores of
devoted Christian lives this divine transaction has
been most distinctly noted. It has been signalized
and made for ever memorable by a conscious and definite experience.

The diary of Jonathan Edwards furnishes a
remarkable exhibition of the various stages of the
Spirit's work in the heart. His conversion was
clearly marked ; and at a later period his full consecration and separation unto God not less distinctly.
He gives us this record of a sacred hour :—

"Once as I rode out into the woods for my health in
1737, having alighted from my horse in a retired place, as
my manner commonly has been, to walk for divine
contemplation .and prayer, I had a view that was for me
extraordinary, of the glory of the Son of God, as Mediator
between God and man, and His wonderful, great, full, pure,
and sweet grace and love, and meek and gentle condescen-
sion. The grace that appeared so calm and sweet, appeared
also great above the heavens. The person of Christ
appeared ineffably excellent, with an excellency great

enough to swallow up all thought and conception—which continued,. as near as I can judge, about an hour ; which kept me a greater part of the time in a flood of tears and weeping aloud. *I felt an ardency of soul to be, what I know not otherwise how to express, emptied and annihilated; to lie in the dust and be full of Christ alone; to love Him with a holy and pure love; to trust in Him; to live upon Him; to serve Him; and to be perfectly sanctified and made pure with a divine and heavenly purity."* *

We have heard Edwards called " The Isaiah of the Christian dispensation," profound wisdom and seraphic devotion being so wonderfully united in him. Certainly here is a scene in the great theologian's life which is strangely like that which the prophet has so vividly pictured in his own.† There is the same overpowering vision of the Lord, the same melting of heart before His awful purity, and the same self-surrendering consecration to His service. If the sealing of the Spirit can ever be discovered in the lives of modern saints, we should say that here is a conspicuous instance. And as we hear him preaching at Enfield not long after, when, as he speaks, the impression of eternal things is so powerful that men cling to the pillars of the church, trembling before the impending terror of the Lord, which he so vividly pictures, we exclaim, " Truly, the anointing which he hath received abideth on him " ! Who shall say that if Christ's servants are still " filled with the Holy Ghost" and speak the word

* Works, Vol. I., p. 21.   † Isaiah vi. 1-8.

of God with boldness, the place of assembly will not still be shaken?

As for the great theologian himself, he furnishes a rare example of baptized intellect. His reasoning is a kind of lofty adoration—a magnificent "*Te Deum*" set to argument. The pathway of his thought is often fairly ablaze with love, while his love seems ever to find the highest expression in contemplating the greatness and glory of God. Where others are subdued by the manifestations of divine goodness, his heart seems most melted and his affections most powerfully kindled by viewing the matchless holiness and infinite sovereignty of God. He gives a most impressive example of great powers consecrated and anointed.

Turning from the profound theologian to a youthful student, we find a similar working of the Spirit, and similar exhibitions of power in the Lord's service.

James Brainerd Taylor had been converted at the age of fifteen. Six years after he experienced a remarkable blessing from the Spirit. All his subsequent papers refer to this date as the most important era in his Christian life. This is his account, somewhat abridged, of what then occurred :—

"It was on the 23d of April, 1822, when I was on a visit to Haddam, in Connecticut. Memorable day! The time and place will never, no, *never*, be forgotten! I recur to it at this moment with thankful remembrance. For a long time my desire had been that the Lord would visit me, and fill me with the Holy Ghost—my cry to Him was, *Seal* *my soul for ever Thine.* I lifted up my heart in prayer that the blessing might descend. I felt that I needed something I did not possess. There was a void within which must be filled, or I could not be happy. My earnest desire was then, as it had been ever since I professed religion six years before, that all love of the world might be destroyed—all selfishness extirpated—pride banished—unbelief removed —all idols dethroned—everything hostile to holiness and opposed to the divine will crucified; that holiness to the Lord might be engraved on my heart, and evermore characterize my conversation. My mind was led to reflect on what would probably be my future situation. It recurred to me, I am to be hereafter a minister of the Gospel. But how shall I be able to preach in my present state of mind? I cannot—never, no, never shall I be able to do it with pleasure, without great overturnings in my soul. I felt that I needed *that* for which I was then, and for a long time had been, hungering and thirsting. I desired it, not for my benefit only, but for that of the Church and the world. *At this very juncture I was most delightfully conscious of giving up all to God. I was enabled in my heart to say, Here, Lord, take me, take my whole soul, and seal me Thine—Thine now and Thine for ever.* 'If Thou wilt Thou canst make me clean.' Then there ensued such emotions as I never before experienced. All was calm and tranquil— and a heaven of love pervaded my whole soul. I had a witness of God's love to me and of mine to Him. Shortly after I was dissolved in tears of love and gratitude to our blessed Lord. The name of Jesus was precious to me; 'Twas music in my ear.' He came as King, and took full possession of my heart; and I was enabled to say, ' I am crucified with Christ; nevertheless I live; yet not I, but Christ liveth in me.' Let Him, as King of kings and Lord of lords, reign in me, reign without a rival for ever." *

* "Memoir," pp. 86, 87.

The invariable accompaniment of such visitations
of the Spirit, we find throughout the whole subsequent history of this young man.   His communion
with God was of the most elevated and transforming
character.   It seemed literally as though it were
Christ for him to live.   For wherever he went he
exhibited the Lord Jesus so conspicuously, in his
example, in his words and in his persuasions, that
men could not resist the power with which he lived
and spoke.   Dying at the age of twenty-eight, his
labours had nevertheless been such a blessing to his
generation, that many servants of God, living till
threescore and ten, might be glad to leave behind
them such a record.   His college and seminary
vacations were spent in evangelistic labours, and
during these seasons he toiled like an apostle.
Night and day with tears he warned men.   Publicly
and from house to house he exhorted, and entreated,
and prayed.   And wherever he went, revivals seemed
to break forth as though he carried some resistless
divine influence in his person, and hundreds in a
town would be converted during a single visit.   His
own soul meanwhile lived in the most exultant
fellowship with the Father and the Son.   He makes
the same record that Edwards does, that the one
memorable season of divine visitation was followed
by many others, in which the tides of heavenly love
and delight filled and flooded the soul.   The joy of
that first baptism and its accompanying power
remained unto the end.

Undoubtedly the regeneration of the Spirit and the enduement of the Spirit are often embraced in a single experience.* Christian Eddy, who lived to prove so remarkably how the faithful house servant and the illustrious saint may be combined in one, gives an example of this experience. She says artlessly—"*At my conversion it seemed as though the Dove rested on my heart, and He has never left me since!*" † So they also thought, thou true yoke-fellow of Christ, who beheld thy holiness and steadfastness in the gospel. If the gift to win the hardest and most hopeless sinners to Christ, and amid all rebuffs to keep the crown of meekness unsullied, be not an evidence of the baptism and abiding of that Spirit which descended like a dove and rested in power upon the Lord, we know not where such evidence could be found. The career of this Cornwall servant is a sufficient demonstration, if any were needed, that the highest endowments of the Spirit are not alone for the eminent theologian and the deeply instructed saint. So is the history of William Carvosso, the humble fisherman on the coast of England. He had not learned to write his name till after he was sixty-five years of age. But at twenty-one the Lord wrote upon him his new

* "Both gifts came upon St. Paul at once—the indwelling of the Holy Ghost and the enduement for service. This was so with him, but individuals have different experiences in that regard. Often the enduement comes later than conversion, because it was not sought at the time of conversion."—*Dr Andrew Bonar.*

† "Consecrated Women," p. 231.

5

name. One year after, he records that he was
visited with a gracious anointing of the Spirit. He
had wrestled in secret places for the power of the
Lord to come upon him, and on March 13th, 1772,
in a little prayer meeting, he relates that a most
blessed experience was granted him. He says:—

"Now I felt that I was nothing and Christ was all in all.
Him I now cheerfully received in all His offices—my
Prophet to teach me, my Priest to atone for me, my
King to reign over me. Oh, what boundless happiness
there is in Christ! and all for such a poor sinner as I."

The evidence that he at this time received a
special effusion of the Holy Ghost is very strong,
for he became henceforth one of the most successful
fishers of men that the Church in latter times has
seen. A sketch of his devoted life records that "at
one place, Cambuslang, where he went from house
to house through the day, and held class-meetings at
night, seven hundred or more were hopefully converted to God."

We have cited these two examples, which might
be greatly multiplied, to show how the humblest
instruments, when filled with the Spirit, are lifted to
the same plane with the mightiest.

In being introduced somewhat into the private
history of eminent revivalists, we have the strongest confirmation of the view which we are advocat-
ing in this chapter. Almost all of them carry the
cherished secret of some special divine visitation by

which they have been empowered for their work.
There are men upon whom no ordaining hands have
been laid, whose success might well be the envy of
the most honoured ministers, if envy were allowed
in such a field. The most painful experience of the
ordinary pastor is the lack of direct results—so
many sermons to which there is no response, and
from which there is no visible impression. Say
what we will about the educating power of the
pulpit, there ought to be no such fixed gap between
ministerial effort and spiritual success. Every good
workman, whether merchant, mechanic, farmer,
builder, or student, is able to see the definite issues
of his toil at the end of the year. So ought the
"workman that needeth not to be ashamed," whom
the Scriptures commend. He should use his sermon
as a means to a definite end—the converting and
sanctifying of souls—and should be disappointed if
he fails to see this end attained. The evangelist
labours on this principle, and often reaps immense
harvests. Has He any secret to communicate to
pastors? Sometimes He has. We will refer to one
who has been used of God to turn thousands to
the obedience of the faith. In a season of confi-
dential communion with brethren and fellow-workers,
he narrated this experience which was taken down
from his lips :—

"It was in connection with evangelistic services which
I was conducting in Scotland in the early part of my
ministry, that I experienced a marked visitation of God's

Spirit. While preaching one evening there fell on me suddenly such an overpowering impression of the realities of the world to come as I had never known before. It seemed as though hell opened to my gaze, and I saw the misery of the lost in all its unutterable woe, while heaven, at the same time, revealed its glories to me so that I apprehended something of the unspeakable blessedness of the redeemed of Christ in glory. So powerful was the impression that I was overcome with weeping, and in spite of all my efforts at restraining my emotion was compelled to retire from the church. In my room alone for hours the visitation continued. I lay there weeping and bewailing before the Lord, that I had loved Him so little and served Him so coldly. I was led after awhile to give myself away to Him in an everlasting covenant. I prayed that He would just take me and empty me utterly of self and fill me with His Spirit. I gave myself up to Him to be despised and rejected and counted a fool for His sake, if I might be the means thereby of saving perishing souls. Never has the memory of the hour left me ; never can it leave me."

In labouring with this devoted servant of Christ, we have always been struck with the fixed relationship between effort and result in his ministry. Oftentimes when the sermon has appeared very ill adapted to the end, the effect has been greatest ; and what have seemed, humanly speaking, the weakest efforts, have often fallen with unaccountable power upon the hearts of the hearers. It certainly is a reiteration of a lesson which we are very slow to learn, that it is " not by might, nor by power, but by My Spirit, saith the Lord." If the preacher's message is made a medium of the Spirit, and not a work of art, it

will not be strange to find the most artless, homely,
and unstudied utterance often carrying the mightiest
results. John Livingstone, the renowned Scots
worthy, says : "There is sometimes somewhat in
preaching that cannot be ascribed either to matter
or expression, and cannot be described what it is or
from whence it cometh, but with a sweet violence it
pierceth into the heart and affections and comes
immediately from the Lord ; but if there be any
way to obtain such a thing it is by the heavenly
disposition of the speaker." No wonder at his comment on the "sometimes somewhat in preaching,'
when the Lord had put on him the signal honour of
bringing five hundred souls to repentance under a
single sermon, and that, moreover, an unstudied and
almost unpremeditated effort. But here, too, the
secret is an open one, for the closet door stands
ajar, and behind the pulpit we catch a glimpse of
an all-night prayer-meeting, in which the preacher
was a participant—a prayer-meeting directed to this
single end, of getting the enduement of power upon
him who should plead with sinners on the coming
day.* Ah, what a mighty make-weight in the scale

---

* " I never preached ane sermon which I would be earnest to see
again in wryte but two ; the one was on ane Monday after communion
at Shotts, and the other was on ane Monday after communion at Holy-
wood ; and both these times I had spent the whole night before in con-
ference and prayer with some Christians—without any more than
ordinary preparations. Other wayes my gift was rather suited to simple
common people, than to learned and judicious auditors."—*John
Livingstone*, 1630.

of success is the baptism of this invisible, impalpable
Spirit of Life ! Science has perfected a balance so
delicate and susceptible, that when two pieces of
paper hold the scales in perfect equipoise, the writing of your name upon one will instantly tip the
beam and bear it down. So it is when the signature of the Spirit is put upon the heart by the
heavenly sealing. It is a transaction so hidden and
so delicate that its subject may be quite unconscious
of it as it is passing. But it has often changed the
whole poise of one's life, transforming the weakling
into a spiritual giant, so that he who has utterly
failed by the energy of the flesh has gone forth
victorious in the power of the Spirit.

We are inclined to believe that this enduement of
the Spirit has often been confounded with conversion, in the experience of good men. When we
hear that Dr. Chalmers, or Legh Richmond, or
William Haslam preached the gospel several years
before they were really converted, we seriously question the statement, even though these men may
have expressed such an opinion themselves. They
had during these years honestly believed on the
Lord Jesus, and confessed Him with the mouth, and,
therefore, we must think, that had they been called
out of the world, they would have been saved. But
all this time they may have lacked the witness and
power of the Spirit, and therefore exercised a com-
paratively barren ministry. The change which
came to them was so radical and so transforming in

its effects upon their lives that, knowing nothing of
two distinct stages in the Christian life, it seemed to
them like the experience of conversion, whereas we
judge that the difference in their ministry before
and after this change, was quite like the difference
between the ministry of Peter before the day of
Pentecost, and after that day. In other words, the
event from which they dated such a change in their
spiritual history we conceive to have been their enduement by the Spirit with power, rather than their
conversion. This seems to us a much more rational
and scriptural explanation of their experience than
the view, that during all the period before this
striking change they were lost souls and without
part or lot in the salvation of Christ.

We give a single illustration of a transaction
which we regard as belonging to this class. G. V.
Wigram was held in great esteem in the body
known as " The Brethren " for his rare gifts and
remarkable conversation. For several years a com-
municant, and in the judgment of one who knew him
intimately, " a quickened soul," living morally but
without a conscious sense of the presence of Christ,
there fell upon him one evening a powerful mani-
festation of the Spirit. He was kneeling at his
bedside, absent-mindedly saying his prayers, when,
he says,

"Suddenly there came on my soul a something I had
never known before. It was as if some One Infinite and
Almighty, knowing everything, full of the deepest, tenderest

interest in myself, though utterly and entirely abhorring
everything in and connected with me, made known to me
that He loved myself. My eye saw no one, but I knew
assuredly that the One whom I knew not and had never
met, had met me for the first time and made known to me
that we were together. There was a light that no sense
or faculty my own human nature ever knew; there was a
presence of what seemed infinite in greatness—something
altogether of a class that was apart and supreme, and yet at
the same time making itself known to me in a way that I as
a man could thoroughly feel, taste, and enjoy. The Light
made all light, Himself withal ; but it did not destroy, for it
was love itself, and I was loved individually by Him. The
exquisite tenderness and fulness of that love, the way it
appropriated me myself for Him in whom it all was, while
the light from which it was inseparable in Him, discovered
to me the contrast I had been to all that was light and
love. I wept for a while on my knees, said nothing, then
got into bed. The next morning's thought was, 'Get a
Bible.' I got one, and it was thenceforward my hand
book."*

This graphic experience we do not dwell upon in
order to emphasize the marvellous element in it,
though it was so intense that its subject referred to
it till his dying day with the deepest emotion. The
fact on which we would lay special stress is that
from that hour this man was utterly given up to
Christ. He laid his large fortune at the feet of Jesus,
spending thousands yearly for the furtherance of the
gospel, reserving nothing for himself but the pilgrim's
portion, food and raiment. His spiritual gift was

* " The Ministry of G. V. Wigram," Introduction.

not that of evangelist, but of teacher, and in this
office he greatly enriched all that sat under his
instruction.   His ministry, says a co-labourer, " like
the precious stones on Aaron's breast-plate, sparkled
with the varied beauties and glories of the person of
the living and glorified Christ."   And considering that
this ministry, with its extraordinary consecration and
light, dated from that single bedside experience when
he knelt in tears before the Lord, it will not seem
strange if we scrutinize that experience to discover,
if possible, its true interpretation.   However, let us
say distinctly, and let us underscore the statement,
that we have not brought forward any of these remarkable spiritual exercises as models for other
Christians to copy.   Only it is needful sometimes,
in setting forth an obscure truth, to print our argument in illuminated text in order to win attention
for it.   Afterwards it will be easily read in common type.   That is to say, it often requires the
most vivid and powerful experiences to impress us
with the reality of a certain doctrine, which, after
we have once accepted, we can discover in its most
ordinary manifestations.   We believe that scores
in our times have experienced the sealing of the
Holy Spirit who can speak of no extraordinary
emotion connected with the event.   They have
received the power from on high and the witness
within, and yet they have hardly known when or
where these came to them.   What we would urge
is that there is an anointing of the Spirit for service

to which many of us are strangers, and that it is our privilege to seek it with all the heart. How large a proportion of professed Christians, if they were asked, would have to confess that they have never led a soul to Christ. And yet they are true believers, and will doubtless be saved at last—saved but unrewarded ; fitted to "enter into life," but not to enter into the highest "joy of the Lord " ; redeemed through the finished work of Christ, but having no finished work of their own, concerning which the Master can say, " Well done, good and faithful servant."

In view of the fearful possibility of being found in such a condition, we trust that our readers, instead of turning aside from the teaching of this chapter, and perchance condemning it as high or mystical or visionary, may be moved to pray with an open and hungry heart that if there be any deeper work and any mightier communication of the Spirit than they have known, it may be granted unto them. And we are most deeply assured, that if in all humility and self-surrender such a blessing be sought, it will be found. Ecstacies and raptures the Lord may not choose to give us, nor are these needed. But His Holy Spirit's fulness and power He will give us, if we reverently and patiently seek for it.

SONSHIP AND COMMUNION.

"SONSHIP being founded on resurrection, stands connected with perfect justification—perfect righteousness—perfect freedom from everything that could in anywise be against us. God could not have us in His presence with sin upon us. The father could not have the prodigal at his table with the rags of the far country upon him. He could fall on his neck and kiss him in those rags. It was worthy and beautifully characteristic of his *grace* to do ; but then to seat him at the table in rags would never do. The grace that brought the father out to the prodigal reigns through the righteousness which brought the prodigal in to his father. It would not have been grace, had the father waited for the son to deck himself in robes of his own providing ; it would not have been righteousness to bring him in in his rags ; but both grace and righteousness shone forth in all their respective brightness and beauty when the father went out and fell on the prodigal's neck, and yet did not give him a seat at the table until he was clad and decked in a manner suited to that happy position. God in Christ has stooped to the very lowest point of man's moral condition, that by stooping He might raise man to the very highest point of blessedness in fellowship with Himself."—*C. H. M.*

V.

SONSHIP AND COMMUNION.

IT is all-important that we should understand the exact relationship of these two facts. Sonship is not acquired through communion with God ; but communion with God is the issue and fruit of sonship. So many persons reverse the divine order, and think to secure a standing with the Father by the intensity of their spiritual exercises, and the consistency of their Christian walk, that it is needful to make this point very clear. "*But as many as received Him* to them gave He power to become the sons of God, even to them *that believe on His name*."* "For ye are all the children of God *by faith in Christ Jesus*."† Thus speaks the Scripture, and thus are we taught that it is faith in Christ, and not feeling in ourselves, that constitutes us the sons of God. "Whosoever believeth that Jesus is the Christ is born of God."‡

This relation of sonship being once established, through our personal faith, it becomes a fixed fact. Communion varies ; sonship is unchangeable ; communion is a thing of degrees ; sonship is absolute.

---

* John i. 14.   † Gal. iii. 26.   ‡ 1 John v. 1.

The most exalted saint is no more a child of God than the weakest and most imperfect believer. The difference between the two is a difference of fellowship, and not a difference of birthright. Our acceptance with God does not lie along a sliding scale of frames and feelings, but is grounded on the unchangeable life and love of Him who is " the same yesterday, and to-day, and for ever." Those who savingly believe therefore are the sons of God without condition, and all stand on exactly the same plane of acceptance and privilege in the household of faith. A child may be disobedient, but he does not thereby cease to be his father's son ; and a Christian may lose his joy and his assurance, but that does not cancel his birthright and throw him back into spiritual orphanage. But we must add, lest we should seem to lean towards Antinomian license, that there will be a vast difference in the rewards of the children of God, both as to their present joy and their future glory ; and this difference will depend upon the fellowship and faithfulness which they maintain in their walk with God.

Let us clearly discern the exact connection of these two facts, therefore, and lay a strenuous emphasis on each. " Behold what manner of love the Father hath bestowed upon us, *that we should be called the sons of God* '* If sons of God we certainly have the indestructible life of God. And so in spite of the plausibility of the arguments for the contrary view,

* I John iii. I.

we must still hold fast to the doctrine of "the perseverance of the saints"; or as it might be more
justly expressed, of the perseverance of the Saviour.
Not because faith has the tenacity to hold fast to
the end, but because faith makes us partakers of the
eternal life which holds us fast unto the end. For
how can the eternal life perish, and if that life
has become our life how can we perish ? Adoption
may be annulled, but birth cannot be; and hence
those who have been begotten of God cannot die so
long as God lives. Is there such a thing as becoming
unborn for those who have been newborn ? " I give
unto them eternal life; *and they shall never perish,*
neither shall any man pluck them out of My hand,"
is Christ's promise. And incarnation and regeneration are the two bonds by which He has secured
this promise. For through the first He has become
partaker of our human nature, and carried it up into
heaven; and through the second we have been
made partakers of the divine nature, which, could
we be lost, we should have to carry down into
hell.*

---

* Tauler, the mystic, tells of a poor peasant from whom he gained
deep instruction in spiritual things. To his searching question, " But
what would you say if God should damn you ? " " If God would damn
me ? " said the poor man ; " verily if He would use me so hardly, I have
two arms to embrace ; the one whereof is a deep humility by which I
am united to His holy humanity ; the other is faith and charity, which
joins me to His Divinity, by which I would embrace Him in such sort
that He should be constrained to descend with me into hell, and I had
rather without comparison be in hell with God, than without Him in
Paradise."—*Tauler,* 1290—1361.

But next to the gift of sonship, which calls out
the Apostle's exultant thanksgiving, is that of fellowship. " And truly our fellowship is with the Father,
and with His Son Jesus Christ." In sonship we have
life ; in fellowship we have more abundant life : in
the one we get our place as " accepted in the
Beloved " ; in the other we get our power as anointed
with the Holy Ghost : on the one depends our salvation ; on the other depends our sanctification
Now communion or fellowship implies a reciprocal
intercourse with God. By it we not only abide in
Christ, but Christ abides in us ; we not only ask,
but we receive ; we not only give ourselves to God
but God imparts Himself to us. And the Holy
Spirit is the medium of this communion. As the
atmosphere stands between us and the sun, the
transparent element through which we behold its
brightness, and through which its warmth is trans
mitted to us, so the Holy Ghost mediates between
us and Christ. " He shall take of Mine, and shall
show it unto you," * says Jesus. Here is one side—
the communication of the life and love and joy o
the Lord to us. " The Spirit maketh intercession fo
us."† Here is the other side—the communication
of our needs and sorrows, our praises and confession
to the Lord. And both these ideas are involved in
full communion with Christ.

To establish this fellowship we make use, firs
of all, of the Scriptures, which are the inspired orga1

* John xvi. 15. † Rom. viii. 26.

of the Holy Ghost. And it is very important for
us to see that the most direct and intelligible means
of communion is the word of God. Meditation,
contemplation, aspiration—these are very vague and
unsatisfactory exercises when attempted alone.
Thought, like the vine, needs a trellis on which to
climb, in order to mount up into the sunlight. We
require God's Word as a support and uplift in order
that we may think God's thoughts after Him. And
we are sure that the most substantial and most satis-
factory intercourse which we can have with the Lord
is attained in this way.

Rev. William Haslam, the well-known evangelist,
in referring to that remarkable crisis in his ministry
when he gained the power of the Holy Ghost as he
had never known it before, says :—

"A book came into my hands which interested me
greatly. This I read and re-read, and made an abstract of
it. It was the 'Life of Adelaide Newton.' What struck
me in it so much was to find that *this lady was able to hold
spiritual communion with God by means of a Bible only.* Is
it possible, I thought, to hold such close communion with
the Lord apart from the Church and her ministrations? I
do not hesitate to say that this was the means under God of
stripping off some remains of my grave-clothes, and enabling
me to walk in spiritual liberty." *

The lady to whom he refers was one of the excellent of the earth, in whom we may believe the
Lord delighted. Her expositions of Hebrews and

* "From Death Unto Life," p. 59.

of the Song of Solomon are among the best speci-
mens of devotional study with which we are acquainted.   Here we find affection and meditation
climbing up to the Lord along His promises and
precepts.   And as we read, we learn the true secret
of communion.   Unsustained contemplation soon
tires ; but that which mounts up to God along
the *scala sancta* of Scripture renews its strength at
every step.   It has such secure foothold that it never
falters or grows dizzy ; and thus it escapes the
peril of fanaticism and pious dreaming.   " For as
the heavens are higher than the earth, so are My
ways higher than your ways, and *My thoughts than
your thoughts,"* * saith the Lord.   We cannot reach
God's thoughts, therefore, by meditation or reflection
alone.   We may tarry all night in the fields like
Jacob, but unless we know the Scriptures we have
not the ladder whose top reaches unto heaven,
along which our thoughts like angels may ascend
and descend.

And next to God's recorded thoughts, the highest aid to communion will be found in the spiritual
contemplations of His saints.   Each believer needs
the help of every other in order to any measure of
apprehension of God.   " That ye may be able to
comprehend *with all saints* what is the breadth, and
length, and depth, and height, and to know the love
of Christ which passeth knowledge,"† is the fervent
prayer of the Apostle.   Each son of God has some

---

* Isaiah iv. 8.   † Eph. iii. 18.

vision and apprehension of the Father's will and glory which another may miss. And we require the sum of all Christian knowledge to help us toward the beginning of that which " passeth knowledge."

It has sometimes struck us as being one of the saddest fruits of schism in the Church, that it has begotten a kind of covetousness of truth and love. Christians hold their favourite doctrines as a sort of spiritual monopoly ; loving truth for the distinction it may give to them, as the miser loves his gold, instead of loving it for the blessing and joy it may bring to others when imparted. To find the highest help in communion we must be willing to give all we have without stint ; and to take from all who have acquired any riches of truth, however remote and out of ecclesiastical fellowship with us they may be. We make good our suggestion by borrowing from one whom we must own as a true saint, though found within the pale of an apostate body. Fenelon, shut up within the bounds of a narrow and exclusive Church, deprecated what he calls " the avarice of prayer," and not less the avarice of communion. With a most comprehensive charity he exclaims :—

" Oh ! how blessed it were to see ' all goods in common,' both of mind and of body, and that every one no longer regarded his thought, his opinions, his science, his light, his virtues, his noble sentiments, as his own. It is thus that the saints in heaven have all in God, and nothing for themselves alone. Theirs is a beatitude infinite and common to all, of which the ebb and flow cause the abundance and satiety of all the blessed ; each receiving his measure, each giving out all he has received.   If men here below entered into this poverty of spirit and this community of spiritual gifts, we should see all disputes and all schisms come to an end.   We cannot reform the Church except by thus reforming ourselves; then all would be only one spirit ; the spirit of love and truth would be the soul of the members of the body of the Church, and would re-unite them in closest bonds.   It would be a commencement of the new creation, of the   paradise reserved for the world to come."

Probably it is the very highest attainment in prayer to gain real   and sensible communications from   the   Lord.   How few of us know very much of such experiences !   We ask, and having soon exhausted the list of our requests, we give over asking.   We know little of that importunate " I will not let Thee go except Thou bless me."   And when we read, for example, of Bishop Andrewes spending the greater part of five hours every day in prayer and devotion ; or of John Welsh who thought that day ill spent which did not witness eight or ten hours of closet communion, we ponder with amaze-ment, if not with incredulity ; and we ask ourselves how such prolonged   praying   could   be   possible without falling into an endless routine of vain repeti-tion.   So far as we can know, that which these men sought was communion.   They were not merely begging something of God, and persisting in their suit till they should overcome His reluctance. They were seeking contact, fellowship, oneness of mind and will with the Lord ; they were gazing into the face of the Holy One, that so the divine transformation into His likeness might go on ; they were striving by patient endurance to apprehend that for which they were apprehended of Christ Jesus ; laying hold of God and giving themselves to be laid hold of by God. It is good for us to search for the secret of such communion, or at least to be quickened by it to a more prayerful life. How our careless intercessions are rebuked by a passage like this from the life of that excellent Covenanter, Robert Bruce. Says John Livingstone :—

"Upon one occasion I went to Edinburgh to see him in company with the tutor of Bonnington. When we called at eight in the morning, he told us he was not inclined for company; and on being urged to tell us the cause, he answered that when he went to bed he had a good measure of the Lord's presence, but *that he had wrestled about an hour or two before we came, and had not yet got access;* * and so we left him."

Here is a bit of spiritual history so antique and strange that we almost need an interpreter to translate it into the dialect of common experience. How many Christians have prayed for years without ever having striven to get "access," or even known that such a thing were possible.

A communion, we have observed, in which something is imparted from God to us as well as some-

* "Scots Worthies," p. 159.

thing asked of God by us, should be constantly
sought. Is it possible for the Lord, through the
Holy Spirit, to make direct and intelligible communications to our spirits, instructing us in regard
to duty, and clearly enlightening us respecting His
will ? Certainly, Christians who have sought to
read God's handwriting from the tablet of consciousness, have often been deceived and led into
grievous mistakes. This fact should be admitted
and marked for our warning and admonition, as
should also the supplementary fact that the Holy
Scriptures are the great and principal manual of
instructions for Christian duty. But there are
emergencies when we need more minute and specific
directions than could possibly be contained in so
general a book. And certainly the Holy Spirit does
give these to those who wait upon Him. But how ?
We should say generally by a providential guidance.
If we seek submissively and humbly to be directed
by the Spirit, we shall be so led, though we may
not know the way beforehand. That is to say, the
Spirit within the believer will rather incline him to go
in the right way, than say distinctly to his inner ear,
" This is the way, walk ye in it." The author of the
Theologia Germanica states this idea truly, though
somewhat extremely, when he says that one who
is led by the Spirit is " so possessed by the
Spirit of God that he does not know what he doeth
or leaveth undone, and hath no power over himself ;
but the will and Spirit of God has the mastery

over him, and works and does and leaves undone with him and by him as God would." Besides this we must believe that to obedient and humble souls the Master does sometimes speak in distinct tones, through the Spirit. But it is only to " a mind inwardly retired before the Lord " that this privilege is given ; it is only ears made divinely sensitive by long communion with Christ, that can catch His still small voice as it speaks in the depths of the heart.

For instruction on this point let us refer to a single teacher. Catherine of Siena, that pearl of piety and purity shining so conspicuously among the corruption of the 14th century, has left us several chapters of her " Dialogue " with God. She explains that the Saviour did not communicate with her by words, but by impressions so distinct and unquestionable that she was able afterwards to write them down. To those who question the reality of such communications her biographer well says : " Go and make the attempt to live a life of prayer such as she lived, and then, and then only, can you have any shadow of a right or any power to judge of this soul's dealings with God." Reading the story of her saintly life, of her consecration so simple and so free from the superstitions of her age, we are inclined to think that God would be as likely to speak to her as to any whom we could name. And interposing again a warning against trusting to mere impressions, we may still ask : if "*the Spirit said to Philip,* Go near and join thyself to this chariot"; if "*the Spirit said, Separate Me Saul and Barnabas,*" why may not the same Spirit speak to Christians to-day who are living under the same dispensation?

Catherine had at one time spent three days in a solitary retreat, praying for a greater fulness and joy of the divine presence. But instead of this, it seemed as though all the legions of darkness had been let loose in her soul, filling her with blasphemous thoughts and evil suggestions. The battle waxed desperate, and she was sore pressed with fear, till at last the Saviour appeared to her and scattered the hosts of darkness and gave her deliverance :—

"Now a great light seemed to descend from above, filling the place where she kneeled with heavenly brightness. The devils fled, and the Lord Jesus conversed with her. Catherine asked him, ' Lord, where wert Thou when my heart was so tormented ? ' ' I was in thy heart,' He replied. ' O Lord, Thou art everlasting truth,' she replied, ' and I humbly bow before Thy word ; but how can I believe that Thou wast in my heart when it was filled with such detestable thoughts ? ' ' Did these thoughts give thee pleasure or pain ? ' asked the Lord. ' An exceeding pain and sadness,' she replied ; to whom the Lord—' Thou wast in woe and sadness because I was in the midst of thy heart. My presence it was which rendered those thoughts insupportable to thee. Thou didst strive to repel them, because they filled thee with horror, and because thou didst not succeed thy spirit was bowed down with sorrow. When the period I had determined for the duration of the

combat had elapsed, I sent forth the beams of My light,
and the shades of hell were dispelled, because they cannot
resist that light'" *

Here is a most vital lesson for believers. For we
have not only a vivid illustration of the tender and
gracious intercourse, which is possible between the
saint and his Saviour, but we have also a salutary
warning. The hour of holiest communion is not
unlikely to be made the "hour and power of darkness," by the incursions of the Evil Spirit. The
sleepy and stupid Christian, baptized with "the
spirit that now worketh in the children of dis-
obedience," and living in fellowship with the God of
this world, will not be greatly liable to assaults from
the Evil One. It is those who strive for the highest
consecration who will encounter the sharpest temptations. How instructive a lesson for us it is,
that the first chapter in the Saviour's experience
after His baptism by the Holy Ghost opens with
these words, "And Jesus being full of the Holy
Ghost was led by the Spirit into the wilderness,
being forty days tempted by the devil." † Let not
the Christian be surprised, therefore, to find his still
hour disturbed by intruding thoughts and impudent
suggestions of evil. The closet is the Thermopylæ
of the kingdom of heaven ;. and he who with prayer
and fasting attempts to take the kingdom by force,
will find the spirits of evil massed there in strong

---

* "Catherine of Siena," 1347-1380.   † Luke iv. 2.

array to resist him.   Bunyan never penned words
of deeper significance than when he wrote, " Then
I saw that there was a way to hell even from the
gates of heaven."   But He whom we meet in the
closet is faithful, " who will not suffer us to be
tempted above that we are able ; but with the
temptation will also make a way of escape, that we
may be able to bear it." *

With the closest access to God, will come the joy
of the Lord, filling and overflowing the soul.   This
is the true reward and fruition of earnest communion
—a reward which is not to be sought as an end
but which will be certain to follow as a result
How difficult it is to persuade even Christians that
joy in God is the only enduring and really sub
stantial happiness.   Many who truly love the Lord
plead their right to temper and season their Christian
exercises by worldly entertainment.   We urge no
ascetic rule here ; only we wish to remind the
Christian that the love of God is the only love that
can never be inordinate—the only love in which
there can be no hurtful excess.   In this respect i
stands in total and unchangeable contrast to worldly
affection.   Read this confession of the brillian
Madame de Maintenon, which she makes to a frienc
in the acme of her splendour : " Do you not see
that I am dying with melancholy, in a height o
fortune which once my imagination could scarce
have conceived ?   I have been young and beautiful

---

* I Cor. x. 13.

have had a high relish of pleasure, and have been
the universal object of love. In a more advanced
age I have spent years in intellectual pleasures ; I
have at last risen to favour ; *but I protest to you, my
dear madam, that every one of these conditions leaves
in the mind a dismal vacuity."* Turn from this
beautiful court favourite to another French lady of
the same period. Madame Guyon was the most
despised and persecuted woman of her time—
hunted, derided, imprisoned, exiled. But writing of
her spiritual joy at this period, she says :—

*"The love of God occupied my heart so constantly and
strongly that it was very difficult for me to think of anything
else.* So much was my soul absorbed in God, that my eyes
and ears seemed to close of themselves to outward objects,
and to leave the soul to the exclusive influence of the
inward attraction. This immersion in God so absorbed all
things, that it seemed to place all things in a new position
relating to God. I could behold nought out of God ; I
beheld all things in Him."

Let us mark what the Scriptures say concerning
those who are sealed—" Ourselves also which have
the *first-fruits of the Spirit."* * " Sealed with that
Holy Spirit of promise *which is the earnest of our
inheritance."* † This signifies that those who are
filled with the Spirit already have foretastes of
heaven, prelibations of the " pleasures for evermore "
which are at the Lord's right hand. If so, we need
not speculate concerning the blessedness of the

---

* Rom. viii. 23.   † Eph. i. 13.

redeemed.   He who has the handful of first-fruits
knows what the harvest will be just as well as h
will know when the grain has been reaped an
gathered into the garner.   The hearts of the re
deemed above and below beat with the same impulse
and keep time to the same heavenly harmony.   Why
stand ye gazing up into heaven therefore, speculat
ing with curious wonder concerning the bliss of th
glorified ?   Put your ear to the heart of the saint i
full communion with God, if you would know wha
the beatific joy is.   Heaven is perfectly miniatured
wherever you find a soul in perfect fellowship witl
the Lord.

We have spoken in another chapter of the gra
cious visitations of the Spirit enjoyed by Presiden
Edwards.   These were attended by experiences o
the most seraphic delight—experiences in whicl
the weight of glory was such as to cause him " t
break forth into a kind of loud weeping," while h
contemplated the character of God.   Let us hea
his description of this divine enjoyment :

" I found from time to time an inward sweetness tha
would carry me away in my contemplations.   This I kno\
not how to express otherwise than as a calm, swee
abstraction of the soul from all the concerns of the world
and sometimes a kind of vision or fixed ideas and imagina
tions, of being alone in the mountains, or some solitar
wilderness, far from all mankind, sweetly conversing wit
Christ, and wrapped and swallowed up in God." *

* Edwards' Works, Vol. I., p. 16.

But let it be carefully observed that these exercises came from no idle dreaming, no luxurious
spiritual reveries. It was, he tells us, while reading
the Scriptures that his soul so mounted up ; and
it was while his eye was fixed on God that his
heart was kindled with holy delight. Men of this
world talk about enjoying themselves ; the believer's
happiness is most intense when he is out of himself,
so that he can "joy in God through our Lord Jesus
Christ." Edwards has given an extended and glowing narrative of high religious joy in another person
with whom he was intimate ; and who, though no
name is mentioned, has been ascertained since his
death to have been his own wife. We can give only
a few snatches from this wonderful record of blessedness. If we wished for a living commentary upon
John Howe's lofty discourse on " Delighting in God,"
we should select this. It is the theologian's argument set to heart-music ; and it is especially
interesting as being the manifest fruit of earnest
consecration, and definite sealing by the Spirit.
' *Desire is love in motion ; love is desire at rest,*" says
Howe. Here was a soul who desired God above all
other things. This desire expressed itself in the
most searching self-surrender ; and the delight
which followed was this desire finding rest in its
supreme object. These exercises begun, he says,
' near three years ago in a great increase, *upon an
extraordinary self-dedication and renunciation of the
world.*" The person had been formerly subject to

great unsteadiness in grace and frequent melancholy
But, says the narrator,—

" Since that resignation spoken of before, made nea
three years ago, everything of that nature seems to b
overcome and crushed by the power of faith and trust ir
God and resignation to Him.   The person has remained ir
a constant, uninterrupted rest and humble joy in God, anc
assurance of His favour, without one hour's melancholy o;
darkness from that day to this. . . .

" These things have been attended with a constan
sweet peace and calm and serenity of soul, without any
cloud to interrupt it ; a continual rejoicing in all the work;
of God's hands—the works of nature and God's daily work;
all appearing with a sweet smile upon them ; a wonderfu
access to God by prayer, as it were seeing Him, and sensibl}
and immediately conversing with Him, as much oftentime;
as if Christ were here on earth, sitting on a visible throne
to be approached to and conversed with ; frequent, plain
sensible, and immediate answers to prayer ;   all tear;
wiped away ; all former troubles and sorrows of life forgotten, and all sorrow and sighing fled away, excepting
grief for past sins, and for remaining corruption, and tha'
Christ is loved no more and that God is no more honourec
in the world, and a compassionate grief towards fellow
creatures ; a daily sensible doing and suffering everything
for God, for a long time past, eating for God and sleeping
for God, and bearing pain and trouble for God, and doing
all as the service of love, and so doing it with a continual,
uninterrupted cheerfulness, peace, and joy." *

We have given but a brief extract from this
incomparable narrative.   The reader must study the

---

* Edwards' Works, Vol. III., pp. 302-306.

whole, if he would learn how sober, how orderly,
how balanced with the most practical service all this
exalted communion was.

We have no need to seek for any higher alti-
tudes of spiritual delight than those here pictured.
And yet to show the wonderful manifestations
which God sometimes makes to His obedient children, we may go still further. The experience of
Mrs. Edwards seems to have been a continuous
one, and to have constituted when attained an
habitual state rather than an exceptional trans-
port. But there are loftier peaks looking down
upon the most elevated table-lands of communion—spiritual Pisgahs and Tabors into which
God sometimes calls up His servants that He may
show them His glory. It will not harm us to listen
to the favoured few who have been summoned up
thither, though we may have to discourage others
from attempting to scale such heights. That sublime experience of the Apostle Paul, when he was
so entranced that he knew not " whether in the
body or out of the body," and when he " heard
unspeakable words which it is not lawful to utter,"
was not an attainment, but a rapture. He evidently did not climb to it, but was lifted to it, by a
sovereign and gracious act of the Lord. He was
" *caught up* to the third heaven," he did not go up ;
and from this eminent height he could stretch out
no beckoning hand to his brethren below. But
even these anomalous experiences have their les-

son, especially to an age which is so inclined to
discredit all supernatural intervention. To those
who are blind and cannot see afar off, they open
glimpses of the glory to be revealed, which may
at least give a momentary uplift to the eyes that
are cast down.

John Flavel was by temperament and habit as
remote from enthusiasm as President Edwards.
But here is a passage which he gives from the experience of "a minister," well understood to have
been himself. He was alone on a journey, his
mind greatly occupied with self-examination and
prayer. He thus describes what befell him :—

"In all that day's journey he neither met, overtook, nor
was overtaken by any. Thus going on his way, his
thoughts began to swell and rise higher and higher, like
the waters in Ezekiel's vision, till at last they became an
overwhelming flood. Such was the intention of his mind,
such the ravishing tastes of heavenly joys, and such the
full assurance of his interest therein, that he utterly lost
the sight and sense of this world, and all the concerns
thereof; and for some hours he knew no more where he
was than if he had been in a deep sleep upon his bed."
Arriving in great exhaustion at a certain spring, "he sat
down and washed, earnestly desiring if it was God's pleasure
that this might be his parting-place from this world.
Death had the most amiable face in his eye that ever he
beheld, except the face of Jesus Christ, which made it so ;
and he does not remember, though he believed himself
dying, that he ever thought of his dear wife or children
or any earthly concernment. On reaching his inn, the
influence still continued, banishing sleep. Still, still the

joy of the Lord overflowed him, and he seemed to be an inhabitant of the other world. But within a few hours he was sensible of the ebbing of the tide, and before night, though there was a heavenly serenity and sweet peace upon his spirit, which continued long with him, yet the transports of joy were over, and the fine edge of his delight blunted. He many years after called that day *one of the days of heaven, and professed he understood more of the life of heaven by it than by all the books he ever read, or discourses he ever entertained about it."* *

Not less exalted is an experience of Pascal, which he describes in a paper which he long carried about his person. Dr. Alexander calls it " one of the most seraphic productions of human language." Indeed the visitation described seems to have been so unutterable as to defy full expression. It is joy and rapture breaking through the bounds of speech and expressing itself in tears. So resistless is the tide of love and ecstacy that he can only describe it in such broken phrases as, joy — joy — tears — tears ; " joie — joie — pleurs ! pleurs ! "

But these illustrations are sufficient to set before us the exalted possibilities of communion with the Lord. The degree of our joy and fellowship will vary ; but whatever the degree, let us be assured that such intimate contact with the Lord is of priceless value. Communion with the Sinless One is the only sure method of excommunicating sin.

* Flavel's Works, Vol. I., p. 501.

Gazing into the face of Christ, and beholding the light of the knowledge of the glory of God which shines there, will surely disenchant our hearts from worldly objects. " Ephraim shall say, what have I to do any more with idols ? *I have heard Him and observed Him."* ∗ Dannecker, the German sculptor, spent eight years in producing a face of Christ ; and at last wrought out one in which the emotions of love and sorrow were so perfectly blended that beholders wept as they looked upon it. Subsequently being solicited to employ his great talent on a statue of Venus, he replied, " After gazing so long into the face of Christ, think you that I can now turn my attention to a heathen goddess ? " Here is the true secret of weanedness from worldly idols, " the expulsive power of a new affection."

> " I have heard the voice of Jesus,
>   Tell me not of aught beside ;
> I have seen the face of Jesus,
>   All my soul is satisfied."

Separation from the world, and separation unto Christ, and unto the goodly fellowship of all saints in all ages who are in Christ,—this is the fruit of true communion.

" O Almighty God, who hast knit together Thine elect in one communion and fellowship in the mystical body of Thy Son Jesus Christ our Lord ; grant us grace so to follow Thy blessed saints in

------

∗ Hosea xiv. 6.

all virtuous and godly living, that we may come to
those unspeakable joys, which Thou hast prepared
for those who unfeignedly love Thee ; through
Jesus Christ our Lord. *Amen."*

RIGHTEOUSNESS AND HOLINESS

"THE great marvel of the gospel, the great triumph of redemption is that God can declare to be righteous those who personally are not righteous ; that He can justify the sinner not by deeming him a law-keeper, but even while He judges him as a law-breaker. It is not that being justified by the life of Christ on earth, we are saved by His blood-shedding, but that *being now justified by His blood we shall be saved from wrath through Him as now risen from the dead.*"—*Robert Anderson.*

"TRUE sanctification is the result of the soul's union with the Holy Jesus, the first and immediate receptacle of the sanctifying Spirit ; out of whose fulness His members do by virtue of their union with Him receive sanctifying influence. The other is the mere product of the man's own spirit, which, whatever it has or seems to have of the matter of true holiness, yet does not arise from the supernatural principles or the high aims and ends thereof, for, as it comes from self so it runs into the dead sea of self again, and lies as void of true holiness as nature doth of grace. They who have this spurious holiness are like common boatmen who serve themselves with their own oars, whereas the ship bound for Immanuel's land sails by the blowings of the Spirit."— *Four-fold State, Thomas Boston.*

VI.

RIGHTEOUSNESS AND HOLINESS.

RIGHTEOUSNESS comes before Holiness in the order of redemption, the one being imputed to us on the ground of our faith, and the other being imparted to us by the operation of the Holy Spirit. The way in which we are made righteous is told in the following Scriptures : " But to him that worketh not, but believeth on Him that justifieth the ungodly, *his faith is counted for righteousness.*" * It is a hard saying for the natural man to receive ; and even the Christian has sometimes staggered at it, and tried to mitigate its seeming unreasonableness by arguing that it is by Christ's imparted righteousness, and not by His imputed righteousness, that we are justified. This would mean that we are accepted with God on the ground of personal character, while the Scripture declares that we are " accepted in the Beloved " ; this theory would require us to be made actually righteous through Christ before we could be justified, while the Bible declares that Christ " *is made unto us wisdom and righteousness and sanctifica-*

---

* Rom iv. 5.

tion and redemption." *   In other words, we understand. the word of God to teach that the sinner is
justified on the ground of Christ's righteousness
reckoned to him, and that being thus justified he
is gradually sanctified by the righteousness of
Christ communicated to him.

We can see then the distinction between righteousness and holiness, for there must be a distinction, since the new man is declared to be
created "in righteousness and true holiness." The
one is put upon the sinner when he believes, so
that by it he is "justified from all things"; the
other is begotten within him as he continues to
believe, till he is sanctified wholly. The sunshine
first clothes the dead grass of the field with a garment of light, covering and surrounding it with its
warmth; and then little by little the greenness
and bloom and beauty are evoked out of the dry
stock, as the light is transmuted into life. Here
is a true symbol of justification and sanctification.
Does the doctrine of imputation stumble you?
But "if God so clothe the grass of the field which
to-day is and to-morrow is cast into the oven, shall
He not much more clothe you, O ye of little faith?"
Righteousness with which God covers Himself as
with a garment, He lays upon the sinner as the
first gift of His pardoning grace to cover and en-
wrap him, and then little by little, under the influences of the Spirit, "the beauty of holiness" is

---

* 1 Cor. i. 30.

wrought out from his heart in purity and gentleness and meekness and love, till " Solomon in all his glory was not arrayed like one of these." Justification gives us our title to heaven ; sanctification our fitness for heaven.

The duty of practical holiness we believe needs to be especially and strongly urged in these days. Too many Christians are culpably content with being saved, and take very little thought concerning the duty of being sanctified. And if any are moved to the cultivation of holiness, they are quite likely to be frightened away from its pursuit by the exaggerations and fanaticisms with which the doctrine has been burdened in our times. Indeed, to how many ears does the expression " practical holiness " suggest at once the idea of perfectionism. " The degenerate plant of a strange vine," we hold this to be. The strange vine is the doctrine that regeneration is " a change of nature," instead of the communication of the divine nature. If human nature can be bettered, why may it not be sanctified ? And then, why may not perfection in the flesh be attained ? But because we believe that the carnal man is incapable of becoming subject to God's law, we hold that the believer will never attain perfection until he has put off this tabernacle. It is true even now that the Christian is not in the flesh ; then it will be true that the flesh is not in him, but the Spirit of the Lord will fill him completely and sanctify him wholly.

But does not God command perfection—" *Be ye
therefore perfect, even as your Father which is in
heaven is perfect*"?* Does He not require and
enjoin holiness, " *Be ye holy, for I am holy*"?†
And does He command of us what we cannot perform ? Looking at the question on its human side,
it is enough for us to answer that no man except
our sinless Immanuel has ever performed it ; and
looking at it on the divine side, it is clear that if
God commands anything, He must command perfection—that if He were to fix His standard a
single degree short of this He would not be God.
But looking at both sides, and endeavouring to
reconcile God's claims with man's capacity, we
observe two facts, viz., that in the life and teaching
of Jesus Christ we have the standard of sinless perfection set up, " beauteous as heaven, and,
alas! as remote " ; that above it is the inscription,
" My little children, these things write I unto you
that ye sin not" ; and below it is the superscription ! " *And if any man sin*, we have an Advocate
with the Father, Jesus Christ the righteous." ‡
Perfection is God's perpetual commandment, since
He can require no less ; pardon is His perpetual
provision, since we can attain so little.

Now holiness will be very imperfectly understood, if studied as a mere abstract attribute. We
can learn most concerning its nature and its secret
by seeing its manifestations in the lives of those

---

* Matt. v. 48.　† I Peter. i. 16.　‡ I John ii. 1.

saints who have most signally exhibited it. To take up once more our figure of the light, we know that a sunbeam can only be truly understood as it is refracted by passing through a prism, and so unbraided into its manifold colours. The pure white ray of the divine holiness in like manner must pass through human lives, and be analyzed and reproduced in human virtues, before it can be really apprehended by us. And so we glide from theology into biography—from the idea of holiness to a consideration of its personal manifestations in the saints of God.

If we were to follow strict chronological order in bringing forward our examples of holy living, we should begin with such names as Bernard and Francis of Assisi and Thomas à Kempis. All praise would we give to these devoted souls—the more worthy of our commendation because their light shone amid gross darkness and corruption If the great Arctic explorer was moved to tears at finding a solitary violet blooming beneath an iceberg, one burst of beautiful life amid universal death, our hearts are no less affected at beholding these true saints living so singly for God amid the desolation of Papal corruption and apostacy. And yet in all of them there are traces of asceticism and superstition which render them imperfect exemplars in many respects. Their piety needs to be translated into our Protestant dialect before it can be quite adapted to our imitation ; and there is much of morbid, fantastic saintship which needs to be eliminated from it to render it practical.

Of Protestant saints who have lived excellently for God, where could we find a more illustrious example than in the character of Samuel Rutherford, of whom his biographer truly says, that " he sought for holiness as unceasingly and eagerly as other men seek for pardon and peace " ?   " Upon the bells of the horses ' *holiness unto the Lord,* ' " saith the prophet ; and as this holy man mounts up to God in his chariot of praise, we seem to hear every note in the silver music of pure worship— love, joy, hope, and obedience, and all mingling their strains together in the ' Holy, Holy, Lord God Almighty.' "   We doubt if such words of divine affection were ever penned by uninspired fingers as he employs in setting forth the excellency of Immanuel.   Peruse them, oh soul that would be kindled with divine ardour when your love has long waxed cold.   The sweetness of Paradise is in them, the joy of Beulah thrills in their every accent.   Listen :—

"Brother, I may from new experience speak of Christ to you.   Oh, if ye saw in Him what I see.   A river of God's unseen joys has flown from bank to brae over my soul since I parted with you.   I urge upon you communion with Christ, a growing communion.   There are curtains to be drawn aside in Christ that we never saw, and new foldings of love in Him.   I despair that ever I shall win to the **far** end of that love, there are so many plies in it.   Therefore dig deep and sweat and labour and take pains for Him; and set by as much time in the day for Him as you can; He will be won with labour." *

Consecration is the true fruit of holy fellowship with the Lord. Hence with each kindling of affection, and with each deeper view of the heart of Christ, comes the longing for utter self-devotement. Tired of making his own way and ordering his own plans, he says,—

"Alas my misguiding and childish trafficing with that matchless Pearl, that Heaven's Jewel, the Jewel of the Father's delights hath put me to great loss. Oh that He would take a loan of me, and my stock, and put His name in all my bonds and serve Himself heir to the poor, mean portion which I have, and be accountable for the talent Himself! Gladly would I put Christ into my room to guide all; and let me be but a servant to run errands, and act by His directions—let me be His interdicted heir."

To an unusual degree the heart of this good man was drawn out towards the coming of the King in His glory. His experience in this respect set a deep seal upon the Apostle's words, "We know that when He shall appear we shall be like Him, for we shall see Him as He is. *And every one that hath this hope in Him, purifieth himself even as He*

---

* *Rutherford's Letters*, 1624-1661. "'Rutherford's Letters' is one of my classics. Were truth the beam, I have no doubt, that if Homer and Horace, and all that the world has agreed to idolize, were weighed against that book, they would be lighter than vanity."—*Cecil.*

"Hold off the Bible, such a book the world never saw."—*Baxter*

is pure." The heart is as certainly clarified
under the influence of this blessed anticipation as
linen is whitened out under the shining of the sun.
Holiness is woven into the affections, while love
keeps up the sweet interchange between the soul
longing for sinlessness, and Him who is to " appear
a second time without sin unto salvation." Practise this much neglected apostolic grace, oh reader ;
train faith's eye to " the habit of looking upward
all the day, and drawing down beams from the
reconciled countenance." Waiting for the Son of
God from heaven fixes our position on earth, and
gives us that true separateness and unworldliness
which are so essential to a holy life. He who has
learned to say, " For our citizenship is in heaven,
from whence we look for a Saviour," † has an unan-
swerable reason for not investing his affections or
laying up his treasures on the earth. This blessed
hope has kindled the hearts of saints to the highest fervours, and touched the lyres of poets with the
loftiest strains. ‡ It took such hold of Rutherford that it made him live and act ever as an

---

* 1 John iii. 3.
† Phil. iii. 20.

‡ " I looke for Thee, my lovelyle Lord, therefore
    For Thee I wayte, for Thee I tarrye stylle,
    Mine eies doe long to gaze on Thee my fyll ;
    For Thee I watche, for Thee I prie and pore,
    My soul for Thee attendeth evermore ;
    My soule doth thirste to take Thee at a taste,
    My soule desires with Thee for to be plast."
                        George Gascoigne, 1547.

inhabitant of heaven rather than as a citizen of
earth. Hear his heart's longings after the King
of glory :—

"Watch but a little, and, ere long, the skies shall rend,
and that fair, lovely person, Jesus, will come in the clouds,
fraught and loaded with glory. O, when shall we
meet ? Oh, how long is it to the dawning of the marriage
day ? O, sweet Lord Jesus, take wide steps ! O, my
Lord, come over the mountains at one stride ! O, my
beloved, flee like a roe, or a young hart, on the mountains
of separation. Oh, that He would fold the heavens together
like an old cloak, and shovel time and days out of the way,
and make ready in haste the Lamb's wife for her husband.
Since He looked upon me my heart is not mine own, He
hath run away to heaven with it." *

No holiday sanctity, no holiness of the folded
hands and dreamy heart was that of "Seraphic
Rutherford." He longed after lost souls with the
heart of Christ, and laboured for their salvation
night and day. If he did not say with the Apostle,
"I could wish that myself were accursed from
Christ for my brethren, my kinsmen according to
the flesh," he was constantly declaring that his joy
and rejoicing would be doubled in every soul he might
bring to Christ. To his dear flock of Anworth he
writes : "My witness is in heaven, your heaven
would be two heavens to me, and your salvation two
salvations." Most excellent pattern of godliness !
How our hearts are stirred to emulate his example !

* "Letters," pp. 94, 276.

If we cross from Scotland to France, and study a life which partly overlapped that which we have just considered, we find a type of consecration quite opposite in its character. Rutherford's piety was ecstatic ; Madam Guyon's was mystical ; the one went out of self to the Christ upon the throne and in the clouds ; the other went into self to Christ within the depths of consciousness. Since the Scriptures use the words, "*Christ in you the hope of glory*," we may be assured that the latter method is not altogether erroneous, though from our want of clear vision it may expose us to serious perils. It is a natural experience that souls should find relief in going in an opposite direction from that wherein they have found trouble and sorrow. And we wonder not that after this earnest Spirit had been occupied so long and so painfully with the outward sacraments and symbols of Christ, it should have found glad tidings in the words of a pious confessor, "*Accustom yourself to seek God in your heart, and you will not fail to find Him.*" It would have been false and useless advice to an unrenewed soul. But there is every evidence that this earnest woman had already appropriated the work of Christ for her on the cross and on the throne, and been saved by it. It was the witness and indwelling of the Spirit which she longed for, and yet hardly knew it, and now found : and as in the parallel experience of John Wesley, it was this which henceforth furnished the secret of abounding joy and abounding service. What a change was thus wrought, we learn from her own words :—

These words were to me like the stroke of a dart which pierced my heart asunder. I felt at this instant deeply wounded with the love of God—a wound so delightful that I desired it might never be healed. These words brought into my heart what I had been seeking so many years, or rather they made me discover what was there, and which I did not enjoy for want of knowing it. Oh my Lord, Thou wast in my heart and demanded only the turning of my mind inward to make me feel Thy presence. Oh infinite Goodness, Thou wast so near, and I ran hither and thither seeking Thee, and yet found Thee not. My life was a burden to me, and my happiness was within myself. I was poor in the midst of riches, and ready to perish with hunger near a table plentifully spread and a continual feast ! Oh Beauty ancient and new, why have I known Thee so late ! Alas ! I sought Thee where Thou wast not, and did not seek Thee where Thou wast. It was for want of understanding these words of Thy gospel, ' The Kingdom of God cometh not with observation, neither shall they say *Lo ! here, or lo ! there ! for behold the kingdom of God is within you.*' This I now experienced since Thou didst become my King and my heart Thy kingdom, where Thou dost reign a Sovereign and doest all Thy will." *

The fruit of this divine baptism is what it will especially interest us to seek. And this was immediate and blessed. Will the Spirit that cleanses us from sinfulness also keep us from sinning ? is a question which is asked with the most painful

* " Life of Madame Guyon," by Prof. T. C. Upham, D.D., pp. 52, 53.

solicitude by the tempted, oft defeated and well-nigh despairing believer. The Scriptures certainly give some very strong and explicit promises on this point. " Walk in the Spirit, and *ye shall not fulfil the lusts of the flesh,*" * says the Apostle. And surely there are those who have had glimpses of fulfilment given to them as they have tested this declaration ; who have known what it is to be lifted for the time‑being above the entanglements of "fleshly lusts which war against the soul." If they have not gained full victory, they have at least enjoyed " the truce of God " for a season. There has been a cessation of hostilities, a divine restraint laid upon carnal desires, so that they have been for a time quite subjected to the law of the Spirit. Alas! that such experiences, if they have come, have so often been but transient exercises, not a permanent condition. A sudden misstep and we have stumbled and fallen ; and ceasing to walk in the Spirit, the flesh has again triumphed. If we could only walk always in the Spirit! Oh, but there is the difficulty. " In Him is no sin ; *whosoever abideth in Him sinneth not,*" † writes the Apostle John. If we were in such unbroken communion with Him that there were an unceasing flow of the divine life through our souls, sin would be overborne, quenched, and destroyed. This experience of perpetual walking with God and perpetual abiding in Christ, is the one into which the

* Gal. v. 16.   † 1 John iii. 6.

Holy Ghost is seeking to bring the believer. And it is certainly reasonable to expect that a marked enduement of the Holy Ghost would issue in definite experiences of overcoming. Hear what this pious woman says of that which followed this baptism of the Spirit :—

"I slept not all that night, because Thy love, O my God, flowed in me like delicious oil, and burned as a fire which was going to destroy all that was left of self in an instant. I was all on a sudden so altered, that I was hardly to be known either by myself or others. *I found no more those troublesome faults or that reluctance to duty which formerly characterized me. They all disappeared, consumed like chaff in a great fire.* Nothing was now more easy than the practice of prayer. Hours passed away like moments, while I could hardly do anything else but pray. The fervency of my love allowed me no intermission. It was a prayer of rejoicing and of possession, wherein the taste of God was so great, so pure, unblended and uninterrupted, that it drew and absorbed the powers of the soul into profound recollection, a state of confiding, affectionate rest in God, existing without intellectual effort. For I now had no sight but Jesus Christ alone."

Here is a bright glimpse of the overcoming power of the Spirit.*

We can only judge of the divine side of one's consecration by observing the human side. And when we think of the penetrating, subduing, hal-

---

* St. Theresa of Spain uses very similar language in describing her own experience :—"From the time that the Lord granted me this grace I was saved from all my faults and my miseries. I had power given me to become indeed free."

lowing character of this woman's piety, begetting hatred in some, of course, but conquering so many others and bringing them into obedience to the cross of Christ, it goes far to certify the truth of the above strong statements. Friars, priests, nuns, men of the world, women of fashion, nobles and peasants were drawn to her by a strange charm, and that charm lay evidently in her presence more than in her words. " The unmarried woman careth for the things of the Lord, *that she may be holy both in body and in spirit,*" says the Scripture. And hundreds of Madame Guyon's virgin sisters were immured in convents, seeking thus by retired and hidden communion to become holy unto the Lord. But here was one fulfilling the duties of wife and mother, and yet surpassing them all in her exalted devotion. Like " the holy women in old time who trusted in God, adorning themselves with the ornament of a meek and quiet spirit, being in subjection unto their own husbands," this woman lived and laboured and suffered for Christ. She has been called a Mystic and a Quietist, because she advocated absorption into God, and the stillness and passiveness of the human will that it may be yielded entirely to the Divine ; and theologians have said that mysticism destroys obedience by paralyzing freedom of choice. But life is better than philosophy, demonstration of experience than the deductions of reason. And here was one who in her life shone

like a seraph and obeyed like an angel ; and however we may reason, her own generation and every
succeeding generation has recognized the saint's
halo about her head.　Amid the shadows of superstition which rested so heavily on her times, she is
the one bright figure, who, like the angel standing
in the sun, is not only marvellously illumined
herself, but causes many others to walk in her
reflected radiance.*

The voice of the Spirit is the same in all lands
and in all communions ; and how remarkable it is
that in the heart of John Woolman, the Quaker
preacher, we should find the clearest echo of the
teaching of Madame Guyon, the Catholic saint.
How shall we describe what we feel as we read the
journal of this blessed man ?　We dare not endorse
the verdict of one who calls him " the man who in
all the centuries since the advent of Christ lived
nearest to the divine pattern."　It is impossible to
give such solitary pre-eminence to any disciple of

---

* If she made statements now and then which seem to verge too
near an assumption of holiness, let us read them in the light of her last
will and testament, made just before her death.　It contains this beautiful clause :

" It is to Thee, O Lord God, that I owe all things ; and it is to
Thee that I now surrender up all that I am.　Do with me, O my God,
whatsoever Thou pleasest.　To Thee in an act of irrevocable donation,
I give up both my body and my soul to be disposed of according to Thy
will.　Thou seest my nakedness and misery without Thee.　Thou
knowest that there is nothing in heaven or on earth that I desire but
Thee alone.　Within Thy hands, O God, I leave my soul, *not relying
for my salvation on any good that is in me, but solely on Thy mercies and
the merits and sufferings of my Lord Jesus Christ.*"

—Id., Vol. II., p. 346.

Christ. We have called him above all whom we have known a disciple of the Holy Ghost, and the most worthy exemplar of " the love of the Spirit." Like many to whom we have referred in this volume, he had had his special divine visitation, in which he learned his calling of God. Was it a reverie or a dream which fell on him in deep sleep ? We care not to inquire since we introduce it from no craving for the marvellous, but only for the gracious lesson which it teaches. We give his story, abridged in a few unimportant particulars :—

        " *26th of 8th month,* 1772.

" In a time of sickness a little more than two years and a half ago, I was brought so near the gates of death that I forgot my name. . . . In this state I remained several hours. I then heard a soft, melodious voice, more pure and harmonious than any I heard with my ears before. I believed it was the voice of an angel who spoke to the other angels—the words were, ' John Woolman is dead.' I soon remembered that I was once John Woolman, and being assured that I was alive in the body I greatly wondered what the heavenly voice could mean. I believed beyond doubting that it was the voice of an holy angel, but as yet it was a mystery to me. . . . As I lay for some time, I at length felt a divine power prepare my voice that I could speak, and I said, ' I am crucified with Christ, nevertheless I live ; yet not I, but Christ liveth in me. And the life which I now live I live by the faith of the Son of God, who loved me and gave Himself for me.' Then the mystery was opened, and I perceived there was joy in heaven over a sinner who had repented, and that the language, 'John Woolman is dead,' meant no more than *the death of my own will."* *

He seems to have had a clear conviction of what this signified, and he was "not disobedient to the heavenly vision." For we find him entering at once upon services which only a crucified will would have accepted. At the tables of the rich he bore testimony against luxurious living, warning self-indulgent Christians against pride of apparel and pride of position, and telling them even with weeping that by such things they became enemies of the cross of Christ. With a tenderness which few could wholly resist, he pleaded the cause of the slave against his master, and again and again succeeded in unlocking the bondman's fetters. In trials and tears and hardships he wrought continually till his course was finished, acknowledging that "*this state in which every motion from the selfish spirit yieldeth to pure love*," had been opened before him "as a pearl to seek after." Here, if we will look at it, is a high example of practical holiness—not the sanctity of the cloister or the cell, but that which touched every condition of sin and wrong with its gentle rebuke and its tearful sympathy. And in all these circumstances the purest communion with God was enjoyed. Renouncing wealth he found "that inward poverty under whioh the mind is preserved

in a watchful, tender state, feeling for the mind of
the Holy Leader"; doing that "which subjecteth
the will of the creature," he was "herein united
with the suffering seed and found inward sweetness in these mortifying labours." Most worthy
example for us all was John Woolman. A saint
who never "sainted himself"; a servant of God
who plunged into the world, that like his Master
he might go about doing good, instead of hiding
in some sacred retreat, or immuring himself in the
cloister of his own heart in order to get good.
"Be ye holy in *all manner of living,*" * writes the
Apostle Peter ; and this character furnishes a most
impressive exposition of the precept.   In all manner of life he wrought with holy service ; in do-
mestic circles seeking to supplant the maxims of
selfishness by the law of Christ ; in politics medi-
ating between labour and capital, poverty and
wealth ; in philanthropy putting his shoulder under
the working man's yoke and thrusting his own
hand through the slave's chain as bound with him.
How much the world needs to be reminded of
such half-forgotten lives !   How the Church needs
to be admonished by them that saintliness is
something more than a pale contemplative sentiment ; that it has been and can still be as manly,
robust, and practical as the most strenuous moralist
could wish.

Now holiness is an emanation from God ; some-

---

* 1 Peter. i. 15, R. V.

thing of the divine nature absorbed and reappearing in the lives of the good. But the method of appropriating it varies not a little, different souls finding it each in the different Persons of the Holy Trinity. In Edwards, we behold the saint dwelling on this bare attribute of the Almighty till it becomes inwoven with his spirit—saying "the holiness of God has always appeared to me the loveliest of all His attributes." In Rutherford we see one gazing in adoring affection upon the person of Jesus Christ, while he is "changed into the same image from glory to glory." In Woolman we witness one with eye turned in upon the Spirit dwelling in the heart, and through "a mind clothed with inward prayer" receiving his light and love and purity till he is deeply assimilated to Him. "But all these worketh that one and the self-same Spirit, dividing to every man severally as He will."

We judge it true that holiness is that grace which renders us most like to God. "*After God* created in righteousness and true holiness," says the Scripture. Is such a sentiment as humility possible with God ? we may ask then, since it is such an essential element in the holiness of man. Looking at God as a Trinity we see that it is, and that it is very manifestly revealed. The Son is ever humbling Himself before the Father : " The words that I speak unto you, *I speak not of Myself:* but the Father that dwelleth in Me, He doeth the

works." *   The Holy Spirit in like manner is ever
subject unto the Son :   " *He shall not speak of Himself*, . . . for He shall receive of Mine, and shall
show it unto you." †   Oh blessed example for us,
that even between the persons of the Godhead
there is that holy deference and reverent subjection, which makes each to exalt the other and not
Himself.   May we study the lesson deeply !

And this leads us to borrow still another ray of
light on this subject from a well approved life—
that of the beloved Scotch preacher, Robert Murray
McCheyne—" beloved for the fathers' sakes," we
might say, since more than any other in latter
times he revived among his nation the spirit and
power of the old Covenanters.   He sought for
holiness as for hid treasures, and he gained it in
such manner that his life produced a kind of awe
and anger among formal Christians, so that once
even they took up stones to stone him.   But as in
the beginning, while of the unbelieving " no man
durst join himself " to him, believers in great num-
bers were through him added to the Church.

He recognized more distinctly than any with
whom we are acquainted, that " the highway of
holiness " can only be entered through the valley
of humiliation.   So intensely did he realize this
truth that he was constantly watching lest his
striving for high attainments might become a
snare to him, and that he should be proud of his

---

* John xiv. 10.   † John xvi. 14.

humility and conscious of his consecration. He writes :—

"Now remember that Moses wist not that the skin of his face shone. Looking at our own shining face is the bane of the spiritual life and of the ministry. O for closest communion with God, till soul and body—head, face, and heart—shine with divine brilliancy. *But O for a holy ignorance of our shining.*" *

Is not here a serious suggestion for such as may have been tempted to make professions of holiness? The most fatal temptation, we venture to say, that can be presented to the Christian heart! The light is clear when we look through it at the object of our vision, and are not sensible of its presence ; but if there be something in it of bright vapour or cloudy smoke which attracts our attention, it is evident enough that it is no longer clear. And in like manner it is plain that when our holiness or our humility, instead of being the transparent medium of our communion with Christ, attract our attention and remark, they greatly lack in genuineness and simplicity. Alas! what an omnipresent failing is pride! It is certain to perch on every high attainment like a bird of ill omen to defile it with its presence. Spiritual successes and holy acquirements are no more exempt from its intrusions than temporal. Hear McCheyne again :—

---

* "Memoir of McCheyne," Bonar, p. 118.

"*July 8th*, 1836.

" To-day missed some fine opportunities of speaking a word for Christ. The Lord saw I would have spoken as much for my own honour as His, and therefore shut my mouth. *I see a man cannot be a faithful minister until he preach Christ for Christ's sake*—until he gives up striving to attract people to himself and seeks only to attract them to Christ. Lord, give me this ! " *

This is close dealing. It is self-examination cutting to the quick. Would that every minister of the Gospel might write these italicised words upon his frontlet, or those other words of good Philip Henry, " *Preach Christ crucified in a crucified style.*" In no way probably are our efforts after holiness thwarted, as by the intrusion of self-seeking and ambition into those places which should be filled with Christ only.†

As Michael Angelo wore a lamp on his cap to prevent his own shadow from being thrown upon the picture which he was painting, so the Christian minister and servant needs to have the candle of the Spirit always burning in his heart, lest the reflection of self and self-glorying may fall upon his work to darken and defile it. To show how genuine a trait of holiness this self-repression is,

---

* " Memoir," p. 44.

† We call up John Woolman again to quote his artless words on this point. " I was jealous of myself *lest I should say anything to make my testimony look agreeable to that mind in the people which is not in pure obedience to the cross of Christ.*"

we recall the words of Edward Payson touching
the same point :—

"April 1st, 1806.

"Spiritual pride.   By how many artifices does it contrive
to show itself!   If at any time I am favoured with clearer
discoveries of my natural and acquired depravity and
hatefulness in the sight of God, and am enabled to mourn
over it, in comes spiritual pride with, *Aye, this is something
like.   This is holy mourning for sin; this is true humility.*
. . . What a proof that the heart is the natural soil of
pride, when it thus contrives to gather strength from the
very exercises which one would think must destroy it
utterly." *

Let any who may have fallen into the fatal snare
of claiming to be holy ponder these words.   Here
were two servants of Christ who are believed to
have approached as near the throne as any in
recent times.   But what conviction and self-abhor-
rence did this approach beget.†   As the light of
the knowledge of the glory of God intensified, the
shadows of humiliation deepened more and more.
As it was with Edwards, who in the same sen-
tence wherein he says, that God appeared to him
as " an infinite fountain of divine glory and sweetness, being full and sufficient to satisfy the soul,

---

* "Payson's Memoir," p. 46.

† " From henceforth let us resemble the seraphim, who cover their
faces with two of their wings as expressing their humiliation ; with two
others their feet as concealing their obedient steps from every creature-
eye but their own ; and with the remaining two flying, to execute the
will of God, while they cry one to another, ' Holy, holy, holy is the Lord
of hosts ; the whole earth is full of His glory.' '—*A. Rochat.*

pouring forth itself in sweet communications like
the sun in its glory," adds also, " *My wickedness
appeared to me perfectly ineffable and swallowing up
all thought and imagination like an infinite deluge
or mountains over my head,*" so it was pre-eminently
with these servants of the Lord. In Payson we
have an extraordinary example of the results of
spiritual culture. We may call him the Protestant
ascetic. In his determined pursuit of holiness he
mortified his body to the last degree of endurance.
He prolonged his fasts till his friends begged and
importuned him to stay his severities, lest his
health should give way. And his bodily rigours
were only the shadow of his spiritual. He hunted
sin through all its retreats, unmasked it, chastised
it, slew it with a determination which gave no
quarter. We cannot commend his immoderate
asceticism, by which his health was impaired and
his days shortened. We think also that as in the
case of Brainerd, there was a sombreness in his
piety which is not calculated to win men to a love
of consecration. But oh, for a few present illustrations of such holiness as his! How it amazed
and dazzled men by its excess of brightness! The
anger of the worldling dashed madly against it;
the reproach of Christ fell where the image of
Christ was so conspicuously fixed. But the holy
life triumphed for ever when dissolution set its
stamp upon his brow. Behold him in the cham-
ber of death. His white face is turned calmly

up toward heaven ; his pastoral hands are folded
across his breast ; on his burial shroud is pinned
a paper bearing this inscription : " *Remember the
words which I spake unto you while I was yet
present with you.*" And as the hushed throng
passes by for the last look, it is like the multitude
returning from the cross, smiting on the breast
and each saying to himself, " Truly this was a
righteous man." Payson in his death-chamber at
Portland, McCheyne borne from St. Peter's in
Dundee while the sorrowing multitudes present a
scene of lamentation like the mourning over the
good King Josiah—let us ponder these two scenes,
and be persuaded that with all it has lost, our poor
world has yet an instinct which honours holiness,
and will at last lay upon it its tribute of approval.

Would now that from all these examples of holy
living we might gain a strong incitement to follow in the same way. For holiness is the true
birth-trait and characteristic of the sons of God.
If we are "*partakers of the divine nature,*" we
must exhibit the essential mark of that nature,
which is holiness, or, as the Scripture says, we
must be made "*partakers of His holiness.*" " This
justifies us to be the sons of God, when He hath
taken a slip from His purity, and engrafted it in
our spirits ; He can never own us for His children
without His mark, the stamp of holiness. *Our
spiritual extraction from Him is but pretended unless we do things worthy of so illustrious a birth,*

and becoming the honour of so great a Father.
What evidence can we else have of a childlike
love to God, since the proper act of love is to imi-
tate the object of our affections ? " *

As holiness gives the strongest evidence and
testimony that we are of God and from God as to
our spiritual origin, so it furnishes the best war-
rant of our going to God when our course is finished. "Holiness without which no man shall
see the Lord," says the Scripture. Here or hereafter, it is impossible that the soul should have
any clear vision of God, except through the medium
of that purity which is the most essential element of His nature. "In Thy light shall we see
light "—and holiness is the light with which God
clothes Himself as with a garment. The more of
this we have, the more of pleasant communion shall
we enjoy ; the nearer we shall come to the spirit
of the Most High, and the more shall we know of
Him whose ways are unsearchable. And so likewise in the future. For in the world to come what
would it profit us that heaven's gates were open to
us unless heaven's garment were upon us ? Were
we to be placed there in our native impurity we
should be unspeakably miserable. The eye of
God, under whose gaze all pure spirits rest in
holy delight, would bring naught but torment to
us. We should wish only to escape from His
presence, and to find in the rocks and mountains a

* Stephen Charnock, 1628-1680.

hiding-place from Him that sitteth on the throne
and from the Lamb for ever.

Therefore with all self-denial and communion,
with all putting off of the old man and putting on
of the new man, let us seek to be conformed to
the image of God, "to the end He may establish
our hearts unblamable in holiness before God, even
our Father, at the coming of our Lord Jesus Christ
with all His saints."

PEACE WITH GOD, AND THE PEACE OF GOD.

"BEING justified by faith, we have peace with God;
—that is, we enter into the state of peace immediately.
He is a rich man who has a thousand acres of corn in the
ground, as well as he who has so much in his barn or the
money in his purse. So Christians have rest and peace
in the seed of it, when they have it not in the fruit; they
have it in the promise when they have it not in the possession.
All believers have the promise of rest and peace, and we
know that the truth and faithfulness of God stand engaged
to make good every line and word of the promise to them.
So that though they have not a full and clear actual sense
and feeling of rest, they are, nevertheless, by faith come into
the state of rest."—*Flavel.*

————————

"THE peace of God is that with which God Himself is at
peace."—*Augustine.*

VII.

PEACE WITH GOD, AND THE PEACE OF GOD.

PEACE with God is ours by our simple acceptance of it through faith. Christ Jesus "having made peace through the blood of His cross," our reconciliation with the Father is already accomplished. Faith has only to accept it and rest in it as a part of the Redeemer's finished work. Here is a matter of fact, not a matter of feeling. Faith does not create anything or change anything; it simply apprehends what is and counts it true.

> " The lightning's flash did not create
> The lovely prospect it revealed;
> It only showed the real state
> Of what the darkness had concealed."

"O Lord, open Thou mine eyes, that I may behold wondrous things out of Thy law." The wondrous things are there already—atonement, redemption, peace—all these are accomplished realities, standing for their support alone in the cross of our Lord Jesus Christ. We only need sight to behold them, and a believing trust to rest in them. When after a foreign war our nation had sent ambassadors abroad to treat with the foe and they had returned, only the one word " Peace " was shouted out from the ship that brought them into harbour, and in a few hours all the city was thrilling with joyful congratulations. * It was the truth that a reconciliation had been effected that brought this happy peace of mind to the people ; it was not their peace of mind that brought the reconciliation. In other words, fact supplied the ground for feeling, and not feeling for fact.

" Therefore being justified by faith we have peace with God." The faith which rests on Him who "*is our Peace*"; which trusts in Him who has "slain the enmity, *so making peace*"; which credits Him who "*came and preached peace*" †—this it is which brings a true sense of reconcilement to God. In other words, it is Christ's work for us that gives us peace with God, and not Christ's work in us. Talk we about making peace with God ! That we cannot do, and are not required to do, since the Lord has done it for us already.

" Blessed are the peace-makers, for they shall be called the sons of God." Here as elsewhere our Lord Jesus, the strong Son of God, has the highest beatitude. He is the great Peace-maker, mighty to save because a partaker of God's almightiness, and therefore alone of all the sons of men able to accept God's challenge, " Let him take hold of My strength that he may make peace with Me, and

* " Memoir of Francis Wayland," p. 38.
† Eph. ii. 14, 17.

he shall make peace with Me." * So then our peace *with God* rests solidly and solely upon the finished work of Christ.

The *peace of God* is quite another matter, depending for its reality on the work of the Holy Spirit within us. This is an inward experience, as the other was an outward fact. " Let the peace of God rule in your hearts," † says the Apostle. The holy calm in which God dwells—without fear, without disquiet, without forebodings—can be so imparted to our souls, and by the Spirit of the Lord so translated into our personal experience that it shall become as truly ours as it is His. This is the soul's inward millennium, enjoyed while we are yet in the militant condition. Just as our Master said, " These things have I spoken unto you, that *in Me ye might have peace ; in the world ye shall have tribulation.*"‡ It is God's calm amidst the earthly tumult enabling its possessor to enjoy " the most quiet and peaceful liberty, being uplifted above all fear and agitation of mind concerning death or hell, or any other things which might happen to the soul either in time or in eternity." § " My peace I give unto you, not as the world giveth give I unto you." The world endeavours to effect an outward quiet, Christ gives an inward quiet ; the one seeks rest *from* conflict, the other gives rest *in* conflict. " Thou wilt keep him in perfect peace whose mind is stayed on Thee,

---

* Isa xxvii. 5.   ‡ John xvi. 33, xiv. 27.
† Col. iii. 15.   § Tauler, 1290-1361.

136 PEACE WITH GOD, AND THE PEACE OF GOD.

because he trusteth in Thee." * As the ship's chro-
nometer maintains its stable rest and poise amid
all the heaving and agitations of the vessel, because
stayed upon the solid globe, its double bearings
releasing it from the influence of the ship and yielding it up to the influence of the earth's gravity, so
the believer will be held in quiet, who, letting go of
earthly anxieties, yields himself utterly and without
reserve to the sway of the divine will. As saith the
Scripture again, "Be careful for nothing, but in
everything by prayer and supplication let your
requests be made known unto God, *and the peace of
God, which passeth all understanding, shall keep your
hearts and minds through Christ Jesus.*"† Now this
peace is distinctly named as one of the fruits of the
Spirit; and they who have received the second
blessing of the sealing of the Holy Ghost, have often
entered into this second peace and been filled with
its unspeakable joy.

Let us give a marked example of such an expe
rience.

"*But do you see it in your own heart?*" was the
penetrating question of Mr. Haldane which led to
Merle D'Aubigne's conversion. He saw the doctrine of the new birth theologically and as contained in Scripture ; but as yet he had not known
it experimentally, as written in the heart. And
now, while at the University in Geneva, he tells us
that he sought and " experienced the joys of the

---

* Isa. xxvi. 3.　　　　† Phil. iv. 7.

new birth." Being justified by faith, he had peace
with God ; he knew himself forgiven and accepted.
But still he lacked perfect joy and the peace of
God keeping his heart and mind.

Some years after his conversion, he and two
intimate friends, Frederick Monod and Charles
Rieu, were found at an inn at Kiel, where the
chances of travel had detained them, searching
the word of God together for its hidden riches.
D'Aubigne thus tells the story of what there
passed in his own soul :—

"We were studying the Epistle to the Ephesians, and
had got to the end of the third chapter, where we read the
last two verses—'Now unto Him who is able to do *exceeding
abundantly* above all that we ask or think, according to the
power that worketh in us, unto Him be glory,' etc. This
expression fell upon my soul as a revelation from God.
'He can do by His power,' I said to myself, 'above all that
we *ask,* above all even that we *think;* nay, *exceeding
abundantly* above all.' A *full trust in Christ* for the work
to be done within my poor heart now filled my soul. We
all three knelt down, and, although I had never fully
confided my inward struggles to my friends, the prayer of
Rieu was filled with such admirable faith as he would have
uttered had he known all my wants. When I arose, in
that inn room at Kiel, I felt as if my 'wings were renewed
as the wings of eagles.' From that time forward I comprehended that all my own efforts were of no avail ; that
Christ was able to do all by His 'power that worketh in us,'
and the habitual attitude of my soul was, to lie at the foot
of the cross, crying to Him, 'Here am I, bound hand and
foot, unable to move, unable to do the least thing to get

away from the enemy who oppresses me. Do all Thyself.
I know that Thou wilt do it. Thou wilt even do exceeding
abundantly above all that I ask.'

"I was not disappointed : all my doubts were removed,
my anguish quelled ; and the Lord 'extended to me peace
as a river.' Then I could comprehend with all saints what
is the breadth and length and depth and height, and know
the love of Christ which passeth knowledge. Then I was
able to say, 'Return unto thy rest, O my soul ! for the
Lord hath dealt bountifully with thee.'"

Here indeed was a most blessed experience ; but
not something strange and exceptional in religious
biography. We can trace the same thing under
different names through many saintly lives. The
" inward death " of Mysticism ; the " divine stillness " of Quietism ; the " rest of faith " of the
brethren of the Higher Life—all these terms are
readily translated back into the one idea of the
peace of God ruling in the heart. It is, in a word,
the perfect quiet which comes to the soul which is
yielded up in perfect self-surrender to God. Tauler is constantly describing it as the fruition of
that wonderful second life of his after his two
years' retirement from the pulpit into the cell. " If
a man truly loves God," he says, "and has no will
but to do God's will, *the whole force of the river
Rhine may run at him and will not disturb him or
break his peace.*" In another passage of exquisite
beauty he describes at length the delights and
richness of this experience. It is, as we must
believe, the miniature of his own inner life, though

we might almost suppose it to be a leaf from some angel's biography. This is his language :—

"Christ reveals Himself with an infinite love, sweetness, and richness, flowing forth from the power of the Holy Ghost, overflowing and streaming in a very flood of richness and sweetness into the heart that is waiting to receive it ; and with this sweetness He not only reveals Himself to the soul, but unites Himself with her. Through this sweetness, the soul in its essence by grace flows out with power above all creatures, back into her first origin and fount. Then is the outward man obedient unto the inward man, even unto death, and liveth in constant peace in the service of God continually. That the Lord may thus come into our souls also, overthrowing and casting out all hindrances, bodily or spiritual, that we may become one here on earth and hereafter in the kingdom of heaven, may He help us evermore."

But let us pause to say that we should not dwell on such experiences merely to beget an appetite for religious luxury. Spiritual peace is of little value except as it can reinforce our strength for spiritual conflict. The rest of faith by all means ; but let that rest constitute a centre of activity, not a centre of stagnation. And this surely is the reason why God calls us to be sharers in His peace, that we may be thereby armed for His warfare. Have we noted sufficiently the twofold rest to which we are invited in our Lord's oft-quoted invitation, " Come unto Me all ye that labour and are heavy laden, and *I will give you rest* " * ? Release,

Matt. xi. 28-30.

this means, from legal bondage, from fruitless efforts at self-help, from fretting anxieties, and from the burden of sin. It is rest from labour, even from our own profitless, fleshly endeavours to save ourselves and to glorify God. But our Lord imme- diately adds, " Take My yoke upon you, and learn of Me, . . . *and ye shall find rest to your souls."* Here is the promise of rest *in labour,* as the other was a call to rest *from labour.* The attainment of this is the first and very highest condition of power. And it comes from perfect oneness of will and heart with God. " In him we live and move," and just in proportion as we partake of the eternal repose of God by being centred in Him, shall we partake also of the divine motion of God, and become labourers together with Him. Quiet and not agitation is the source of the highest energy.*

He who entered into rest on the seventh day, having finished the work of creation, is He who "worketh hitherto" and is still accomplishing our redemption, " according to the working of His mighty power which He wrought in Christ when He raised Him from the dead." So it comes to pass

---

* " As opposed to passion, changefulness, or laborious exertion, repose is the special and separating characteristic of the Eternal mind and power ; it is the 'I am' of the Creator as opposed to the 'I become' of all creatures. It is the sign alike of the supreme knowledge which is incapable of surprise, the supreme power which is incapable of labour, and the supreme volition which is incapable of change." —*Ruskin.*

that Christians who are most calm in the conscious
enduement of power, are those who have the
greatest energy to stir others. We find an excellent illustration of this principle in the powerful
ministry of William C. Burns, the eminent Scotch
evangelist and missionary. The effects of his
preaching were often as startling as those of Mr.
Finney, referred to in another chapter. We give
a single instance from his own record. It is the
account of a sermon preached at Kilsyth, July 23rd,
1839:—

" And just as I was speaking I felt my soul moved in a
remarkable manner to plead with the unconverted before
me, instantly to close with God's offers of mercy, and
continued to do so until the power of the Lord's Spirit
became so mighty upon their souls as to carry all before it,
like the rushing mighty wind of Pentecost! During the
whole time that I was speaking, the people listened with
the most riveted and solemn attention, and with many
silent tears and inward groanings of spirit; but at last
their feelings became too strong for all ordinary restraints,
and broke forth simultaneously in weeping and wailing,
tears and groans, intermingled with shouts of joy and
praise from the people of God. The appearance of a great
part of the people from the pulpit gave me an awfully
vivid picture of the state of the ungodly in the day of
Christ's coming to judgment. Some were screaming in
agony, others, and among them strong men, fell to the
ground as if they had been dead. . . . To my own
astonishment, during the progress of this wonderful scene,
when almost all present were overpowered, *it pleased the
Lord to keep my soul perfectly calm.*"

Yes! and this is the demonstration of peace as the other fact was the demonstration of power. "*Stand still*, and see the salvation of God." And they that looked on wondered as much at the calmness of the preacher as at the commotion of the people. Ah! but there is a very significant prelude to this scene of spiritual upheaving. His peacefulness was a calm between two powerful agitations, one in the closet and one in the pews. A friend of his records how the evening before a great field-day, he found him lying on his face in an agony of prayer—"*the source, doubtless, of that holy calm which so struck the hearers on the succeeding morning.*" Thus, once more, through the open closet door we discern secrets which no reasoning would have unfolded to us :—

"Mr. Burns went to his room, and whilst we waited for his coming downstairs to dinner we heard a heavy groan. Thinking he had been taken ill, Mrs. Thoms ran upstairs, and found him lying upon his face on the floor, groaning before the Lord. He had gotten such an overwhelming sense of his responsibility for the souls of that people, that he could then think of nothing else. In his absence of mind he had left his door partially open, which Mrs. Thoms shut, and we did not see him again till late in the evening, when he came for the family worship. His prayer then was one continuous strain of self-loathing and pleading for mercy through the blood of the Lamb of God. It happened that his room was next to mine, and all that night I heard him still groaning in prayer." *

* "Memoirs," p. 546.

It is the old wonderful story repeated of Jacob wrestling with God, taking hold of the divine strength and conquering a peace, until the " thou hast prevailed " and " thou hast power with God and with men " is spoken. The peace of God is the true source of power with men, and real power with men is marked by the most serene quiet. Remember what God says of His servant in whom he delighteth—" I will put My spirit upon him, and He shall show judgment to the Gentiles. *He shall not strive nor cry*, neither shall any man hear His voice in the streets." In other words, the enduement of the Spirit is characterized by tranquil strength and noiseless efficiency. The communion which links us to God's power links us to His peacefulness as well.* Let us insist with utmost emphasis that the peace which we commend shall not be sought for itself. This has been the grave defect alike of monkish asceticism and Protestant quietism. A stagnant peace is sure to breed the malaria of doubt and discontent. That which God calls us to inherit is not of this kind. "Oh, that thou hadst hearkened unto My commandments," He says by the prophet, " *then had My peace been as a river.*"† Like the river which purifies itself by its own motion, which keeps all

---

* " God is a centre to the soul ; and just as in a circle what is nearest the centre is subject to least motion, so the closer the soul is to God, the less the movement and agitation to which it is exposed."— *Gotthold.*

† Isa. xlviii. 18.

the banks green and fertile along which it flows, and which as it widens and deepens takes up the ships of commerce and bears them on its bosom. It is the peace of motion, not of rest; of life, and not of death. Good Thomas à Kempis' counsel to the seeker after peace, that he should find it "in poverty, retirement, and with God," was perhaps the best advice that he knew. But it does not satisfy the heart of one who longs supremely to serve God by serving his generation; and we can understand why a zealous spirit like that of John Wesley should have been repelled by the asceticism of the "Imitation of Christ," while he was led by the perusal of the more practical and humane treatise, the "Holy Living and Dying" of Jeremy Taylor, to dedicate "all his thoughts, words, and actions" to the service of God. There are some things which we may pursue as ends, and others which come to us as blessings attendant upon the search after higher objects. Happiness is the accompaniment of virtue; joy is the inevitable reward of well-doing; peace is the certain fruit of whole-hearted consecration to God. But the moment any one of these blessings is sought for itself, it will lose its sweetness and savour. This principle is most clearly set forth by our Lord in that saying of His, "Seek ye first the kingdom of God and His righteousness, *and all these things shall be added unto you.*"* Now

---

* Matt v. 33.

peace is one of the added things which will certainly come to those who trust Christ with all their heart, and serve their generation with all their might ; but it will constantly elude the grasp of those who pursue it merely 'for itself.

Nothing is said about our keeping peace with God by our toil and striving and watching. The peace of God is promised to keep us. We are not to be over-anxious about it, as though it depended upon our efforts. When Gideon had heard the Lord saying to him, " Peace be unto thee," he built an altar in Ophrah and named it " *Jehovah Shalom*,"* the Lord send peace, and then went forth in the way of duty and obedience. Though he had been very self-distrustful, because he was of poor family and the least in his father's house, and though the weapons of his warfare were very contemptible, yet he soon got the victory and brought this nation into long-continued peace ; so that we read that " the country was in quietness forty years in the days of Gideon." We see that he went forth from peace instead of going forth to seek peace ; the altar and covenant of the Lord were his point of departure. Precisely this is our condition as believers. The cross of Christ, inscribed with " *Jehovah Shalom*," is our starting-point. Having peace with God through the blood of Christ, we go forth to service ; in warfare, in testimony, in toil doing the will of God from the

---

* Judges vi. 24.

heart, anxious for nothing, and fixing the eye only upon the glory of God. Then as the certain income of our obedience will the peace of God be poured into our hearts. The more the spirit of the world gets possession of the Christian, the more of the world's unrest and conflict will he have; the more he is given up to the guidance and the control of the Spirit of the Lord, the more of God's peace will he enjoy, since " to be spiritually minded is life and peace." Let us rejoice then evermore, both in the work of Christ done for us, and in the work of the Spirit done in us.

By the one we get the righteousness of Christ imputed to us ; by the other the righteousness of Christ imparted to us. " And the work of righteousness shall be peace ; and the effects of righteousness, quietness and assurance for ever.'

POWER FOR SONSHIP AND POWER FOR

SERVICE.

"THERE are two schools of doctrine among professing Christians as to the offices and relations of the Lord. The first speaks thus: Any work or office, held by Christ, cannot be held by us; it usurps His right if we pretend to share them. The other, which is the old doctrine, answers thus: If the Incarnation means anything, if Christ and His Church are really one body, all Christ's offices first held and exercised by Him on behalf of men must likewise be held and shared by His members, because He lives in them just as they apprehend that for which they were apprehended. The former view, which I feel assured is a mistake, arises from a misconception of the first great truth of *Christ for us*, to the denial of the greater truth of *Christ in us*, and we His members. The latter opens the riches of the glory of the mystery, which is now revealed, which is *Christ in us*, the hope of glory. The latter is the Church's faith which, however caricatured and abused, cannot be denied without sore loss to the deniers. For this faith confesses the Incarnation, that the Lord still dwells in flesh and blood, and that because He dwells in us, though in ourselves we can do nothing, we can yet do all things through Christ, who is the power in us; and because He is 'the same yesterday, to-day, and for ever,' if He live in us, He will yet do His proper works, in and through those who grow up out of self to live in Him."
—*Andrew Jukes*

VIII.

POWER FOR SONSHIP AND POWER FOR SERVICE.

"AS many as received Him, to them gave He power to become the sons of God," says the Scripture. Christ for us as our life must first of all be appropriated in order that we may stand in the place of sonship to the Father. We do not work for life, but from life ; we do not by our own power attain unto Christ, but we receive Christ in order that we may have power to attain. "*We preach Christ crucified the power of God*,"* says the Apostle. That is, we hold up this external fact of the Son of God bearing our sins and putting them away, and we beseech the sinner to look at this fact and accept it and rest in it. This is the Gospel, and the Scriptures declare that this Gospel of Christ is "*the power of God unto salvation* † to every one that believeth." By no striving of our own, by no energy of will or strength of repentance, can we attain unto salvation. Eternal life is the gift of God, which, when we receive it, makes

---

* 1 Cor. i. 18.   † Rom. i. 16.

us partakers of " the power of an endless life "; it
is not an attainment which we can grasp by the
power of our own finite life. In other words, we
are first of all to accept Christ's life and work and
redemption for us, as that which can alone put us
into relations of sonship and justification and fellowship with the Father.

But to such as have already become the sons of
God, there is a promise given of still greater
attainment,—the power of the indwelling Spirit.
" But ye shall receive power *after that the Holy
Ghost is come upon you*, and ye shall be witnesses
unto Me." Before it was power to become the
sons of God ; now it is power to serve as the sons
of God. And it is very significant to observe how
constantly this kind of energy is connected in the
Scriptures with the Holy Ghost. The power of
the Spirit of God."* " The demonstration of the
Spirit and of power."† "With the Holy Ghost and
power."‡ These are illustrations, which might be
greatly multiplied, of the constant association of
these two ideas. Christ's ascension to the Father,
as we know, was the condition of the descent of
the Spirit ; and concerning this the Lord said,
" The works that I do shall ye do also, and greater
works than these shall ye do, *because I go unto My
Father*."§ Thus the ministry of the Spirit was
announced to be mightier in results than that of

---

* Rom. xv. 19.   ‡ Acts x. 38.
† 1 Cor. ii. 4.   § John xiv. 12.

the Son. This would not seem easy to credit. If
we were ignorant of the facts of science, and some
one were to show us a reservoir of water, and tell
us that this element is capable of three manifestations, liquid, vapour, and solid, and ask us which
would be the most powerful, we might say the
solid form ; and looking at the iceberg, which can
crush a huge ship as you grind a dry leaf between
your fingers, this conclusion would seem to be justified. But science would point at once to the
vapour—so light, so impalpable, and in its finer
forms so invisible, and remind us that this is the
power that is moving our huge steamships, and
drawing our countless railway trains, and driving
our ponderous factories—the greatest motive force
in our modern civilization. The Blessed Trinity
has been manifested to us in two forms in this dispensation. First, He came as the Word made flesh,
the incarnate Lord, with the might of His divine man-
hood, that could silence the winds, still the waves,
open the gates of the grave, and reverse the laws
of gravitation. Is not this the most powerful revelation of God ? " Greater works than these shall
ye do," is His answer. When God comes as the
secret invisible Spirit, like the wind which we cannot see, and cannot tell whence it cometh or
whither it goeth ; and when this Spirit shall dwell
in His fulness in believers, moving their wills, in-
spiring their words and energizing their actions,
then shall be seen the greatest things for the glory

of God and the salvation of souls that have yet been witnessed. It is this gift of the Spirit as a divine power for service and testimony, that we wish to unfold in the remaining part of this chapter.

This special enduement of strength from the Holy Spirit we have already alluded to in a previous chapter. We shall now consider it more at length, as revealed in the divine Word and in human lives.

In the case of our Lord Jesus Christ, there is a distinct recognition of this enduement, as constituting His preparation for His ministry. After the visible descent of the Holy Ghost upon Him at the Jordan, we read that He " returned *in the power of the Spirit* " into Galilee,"* and that he went into the synagogue at Nazareth and read and applied to Himself the words of the prophet, " The Spirit of the Lord is upon Me, because He *hath anointed Me to preach the gospel* to the poor." In the Acts of the Apostles we hear Peter declaring " how God anointed Jesus of Nazareth *with the Holy Ghost and with power*,† who went about doing good and healing all that were oppressed of the devil."

In the case of His apostles, we find a constant recognition of the same fact. " Now He which establisheth us with you in Christ *and hath anointed us is God*," ‡ says Paul writing to the Corinthians.

---

* Luke iv. 14.   † Acts x. 38.   ‡ 2 Cor. i. 21.

"*The anointing which ye have received of Him abideth in you*," * writes John. And these, Jesus Christ and His apostles, we boldly affirm to be our exemplars and models in this as in all other things. And the history of God's Church abundantly confirms the view that those who have done the greatest work for God have done it through the unction of the Holy Ghost and power which was on them.

To some this anointing has come almost simultaneously with conversion ; to many it has come at a considerable period afterwards. The Apostles Petei and Paul furnish types of the two classes. Peter we must suppose to have been a regenerated man when he made his confession, " Thou art the Christ, the Son of the living God." But how weak an apostle for one naturally so strong ; how timid for one so bold ; how inefficient for one so zealous ! Yet after that on the day of Pentecost he had been baptized with the Holy Ghost, he was utterly changed. He who had cowered before a maid and denied his Lord, now preached like a lion and boldly declared Jesus to be both Saviour and Lord, in the face of all His foes. Paul, on the other hand, was the same man from the very beginning,† because his conversion and his anointing came close together. There have been some Pauls in the

---

* I John ii. 27.

† " St. Paul was born a man, an apostle ; not carved out as the rest in time, but a *fusile* apostle, an apostle poured out and cast in a mould. As Adam was a perfect man in an instant, so was St. Paul an apostle as soon as Christ took him in hand."—*John Donne*, 1573-1631.

modern Church, but more Peters ; and we shall cause examples of both to pass in review before us. Let us select from our own times an illustration of a powerful revival preacher.

An eminent authority expressed the opinion some years ago, that probably no man since the days of Whitfield had been instrumental in turning so many souls to God by his preaching as Rev. Charles G. Finney.* Certainly we should not know where to look in recent times to find such startling and overwhelming supernatural results attending the proclamation of the Gospel as those which were witnessed under his ministry. As he went from place to place evangelizing, whole communities would be thrown under conviction at once ; upon his very first utterance the feeling would sometimes be such as "to make the stoutest men writhe on their seats as if a sword had been thrust into their hearts." Hearers who succeeded in repressing their emotion in church would rush home, and unable to contain themselves longer, would fall upon the floor and burst out into a loud wailing in view of their sins." In one place, so utterly abandoned and godless that it had acquired the name of Sodom, he preached ; and as at the close of his sermon he began to apply the truth to the people's consciences, he says, "I had not spoken to them in this strain of direct application I should think more than a quarter of an hour, when all at once an awful solemnity seemed

* Kirk's "Lectures on Revivals," p. 142.

to settle down upon them ; the congregation began
to fall from their seats in every direction and cry for
mercy.   If I had had a sword in each hand, I could
not have cut them off their seats as fast as they fell.
Indeed, nearly the whole congregation were either on
their knees or prostrate, I should think, in less than
two minutes from the first shock that fell upon them.
Every one prayed for himself, who was able to speak
at all." *   And the results were even more wonderful than the impressions.   Vast ingatherings attended
his labours wherever he went.   Of the fruits of one
revival which sprang forth under his preaching, so
judicious an observer as Dr. Lyman Beecher declared that it " was the greatest work of God and
the greatest revival of religion that the world has
ever seen in so short a time, one hundred thousand
being reported as having connected themselves
with Churches as the results of that great revival." †

As we consider the issues of such a mighty
ministry, we naturally ask, What was the secret
spiritual history of this extraordinary instrument
of God ?   An intense personality, a vehement will,
a fearless courage, and a fiery enthusiasm,—these
will be referred to at once by many as yielding the
true secret of his power.   Very efficient as a medium we admit these qualities to be, but utterly
inadequate as a motive force for such results.
Natural qualities are sufficient for natural ends,
but not for supernatural.   Savonarola the man

---

* " Autobiography," pp. 103, 161.   † *Ibid.,* p. 30 .

cannot account for Savonarola the preacher. Nature had withheld from him, they tell us, almost
all the gifts of the orator. But when we read of
his intense and enrapt communion with God, his
unconquerable persistence in seeking the power of
the Highest, till " his thoughts and affections were
so absorbed in God by the presence of the Holy
Spirit, that they who looked into his cell saw his
upturned face as it had been the face of an angel,"
we are not amazed at the character and effects of
his preaching—so pathetic, so melting, so resistless that the reporter lays down his pen with this
apology written under the last line—" *Such sorrow and weeping came upon me that I could go no
further.*"

Finney was a Pauline preacher because he had
a Pauline experience—the peace of God and the
power of God coming to him almost together.
And giving all due consideration to his uncommon
natural endowments, we are constrained to find the
chief secret of his success in his remarkable spiritual history. Let us read this as he has written
it for us.

He had been converted after passing through
powerful spiritual exercises, and immediately after,
on October 10th, 1821, while alone in his law office,
he says :—

"I then received a mighty baptism of the Holy Ghost.
Without any expectation of it, without ever having the
thought in my mind that there was such a thing for me,

without any recollection that I had ever heard the thing mentioned by any person in the world, the Holy Spirit descended upon me in a manner that seemed to go through me, body and soul. I could feel the impression like a wave of electricity, going through and through me. Indeed, it seemed to come in waves of liquid love; for I could not express it in any other way. It seemed like the very breath of God. I can recollect distinctly that it seemed to fan me like immense wings. No words can express the wonderful love that was shed abroad in my heart. I wept aloud with joy and love; and I do not know but I should say, I literally bellowed out the unutterable gushings of my heart. These waves came over me, and over me, one after the other, until I recollect I cried out, 'I shall die if these waves continue to pass over me.' I said, 'Lord, I cannot bear any more.' Yet I had no fear of death. . . . Thus I continued till late at night. I received some sound repose. When I awoke in the morning the sun had risen, and was pouring a clear light into my room. Words cannot express the impression that this sunlight made upon me. Instantly the baptism that I had received the night before returned upon me in the same manner. I arose upon my knees in the bed and wept aloud with joy, and remained for some time too much overwhelmed with the baptism of the Spirit to do anything but pour out my soul to God. It seemed as if this morning's baptism was accompanied with a gentle reproof, and the Spirit seemed to say to me, 'Will you doubt? Will you doubt?' I cried, 'No! I will not doubt; I cannot doubt.' He then cleared the subject up so much to my mind that it was impossible for me to doubt that the Spirit of God had taken possession of my soul." *

Then followed the same results as in the apostolic times. First a powerful assurance of sonship

---

* " Autobiography," pp. 20, 21.

in the inward witness of the Spirit; then power for utterance—such that as he went forth preaching whole neighbourhoods would be seized with deep religious impression at once.

Upon which fact we pause to observe that this is the divine way of quickening men to seriousness and repentance. "Give us a revival moved and begotten by the Holy Spirit, and not one stirred up by the coming of an evangelist," is the cry of many Christians—a demand as reasonable as that your telegraphic message shall be brought to you without the intervention of the wires. The Holy Spirit acts through a medium, the Word of God, and through an agent, the man of God; and it is by Christians anointed and filled with the Holy Ghost, that the Spirit's convicting and regenerating power is brought to bear on souls.

Here, too, in a degree, the Master's example holds for the disciples in all time. John the Baptist had this test of the true Messiah given him. "Upon whom thou shalt see the Spirit descending *and remaining on him,* the same is he which baptizeth with the Holy Ghost." * The abiding and indwelling of the Spirit constituted Christ's power not only for personal service, but for communicating spiritual energy to others. He who on the banks of the Jordan was filled with the breath of God, could breathe on His disciples and say, " Receive ye the Holy Ghost."

* John i. 33.

But when the disciples were baptized with the
Holy Ghost at Pentecost, they no longer possessed
the Spirit by measure. They had now His abiding
presence. He "*sat upon each of them*, and they
were all filled with the Holy Ghost."* Now John
could say to his brethren, "But the anointing
which ye have received of Him *abideth in you*." †
And as with the Lord so with the servants, they
could communicate the Spirit unto others. Ananias is sent to Saul immediately upon his conversion, "and putting his hands on him said, Brother
Saul, the Lord, even Jesus that appeared unto thee
in the way as thou camest, hath sent me, that thou
mightest receive thy sight *and be filled with the
Holy Ghost*." ‡ Peter and John are sent to the
Samaritans as soon as it is known that they have
received the word, and *they laid their hands on
them, and they received the Holy Ghost.* §

Not to enter into the difficult question of the
laying on of hands, this much is evident from
these instances, that it is God's way to communicate His Spirit through human vessels which
have been filled and sanctified for this purpose.
And this fact is not strange or foreign to present
Christian experience. We have the remembrance
of having once or twice come in contact with consecrated servants of Christ, who have imparted to
us a spiritual influence as real and sensible as the

---

* Acts ii. 4. ‡ Acts ix. 17.
† 1 John ii. 27. § Acts xix. 6.

electric shock which the galvanic battery gives when its knob is touched. As impossible as it is that our thoughts should effect the world and stir men to action till they have been incarnated in human speech, so contrary to God's method is it that the Holy Spirit should accomplish His convicting and renewing and sanctifying work except by operating through the tongue and life and energy of living men and women. The mimicry of revivals, effected by the skill of magnetic preachers, we indeed too often see. But that an evangelist, filled with the Spirit of God, should stir whole communities with a sudden and resistless religious impulse, is not a strange fact, but one in perfect accordance with Scripture teaching and precedent. Say not in thy heart, oh cautious Christian, that the revival is not of God because it is brought by a man ; that the divine sovereignty has been ignored and sent to the rear because a human agent appears conspicuously at the front. "When God would save man," says Jeremy Taylor, "He did it *by way of a man*" ; and whether it be salvation or sanctification, the conviction of sinners or the quickening of believers, this is always His method.

But there are various operations by the same Spirit, and the same enduement is given for other kinds of service. Let us take an example from among the Christian philanthropists.

Does one speak too strongly who calls the orphanage at Bristol, England, "the standing miracle of the nineteenth century?" We simply point to the fact of one man sheltering, feeding, clothing, and educating thousands of poor children through a series of years with no funds or resources to draw from except what God has sent him in answer to prayer. And remembering also that the money expended in this work has amounted in all to some millions, we concede at least that it is an extraordinary enterprise. We look at the man who has been the human agent in guiding this vast beneficence, and we instinctively desire to get a glimpse into his closet to discover, if possible, what secret transactions with God lie behind this great public transaction. And here we find the same story which has been told over and over again in this book.

George Müller was converted in 1825 while a student in the University of Halle, but until 1829 he seems hardly to have known whether there be any Holy Spirit. He has graphically told us how in that year, while staying at Teignmouth in England, he was made acquainted with the person and office-work of the Comforter, and how the blessed secret of the Spirit's guidance and illumination and enduement was made known to him. It all came to him now as a divine baptism. Of the joy and exaltation which followed he thus speaks :—

"In the beginning of September I returned to London, much better in body ; *and as to my soul the change was so great that it was like a second conversion.* After my return to London, I sought to benefit my brethren in the seminary, and the means I used were these,—I proposed to them to meet together every morning from six to eight for prayer and reading the Scriptures; and then that each of us should give out what he might consider the Lord had shown him to be the meaning of the portion read. One brother in particular was brought into the same state as myself, and others I trust were more or less benefited. Several times when I went to my room after family prayer in the evening, I found communion with God so sweet that I continued in prayer till after twelve, and then being full of joy, went into the room of the brother just referred to, and finding him also in a similar frame of heart, we continued praying until one or two ; and even then I was a few times so full of joy that I could scarcely sleep, and at six in the morning again called the brethren together for prayer." *

He who four years before had drank of the water of life, now found it " within him a well of water springing up into everlasting life " ; and the third experience began at once to follow—" out of his heart shall flow rivers of living water." How many orphaned lives have those streams since enriched and made glad !

What Mr. Müller discovered in this experience was, that the Holy Spirit can do for us those things which with endless toil and endeavour we undertake to do for ourselves. He will lead us into all truth if we will only let Him, instead of taking philosophy and logic as our schoolmasters. Finding out this, he says, " The result was that

* "Life of Trust," p. 71.

the first evening I shut myself into my room to give myself to prayer and meditation over the Scriptures, I learned more in a few hours than I had done during a period of several months previously." Hear this, ye teachers in the schools of the prophets. Some of us think that you have gone down to Egypt for help in summoning science and metaphysics and rational learning into your class-rooms to furnish you the key of knowledge. "There standeth One among you whom ye know not." Ask Him who has been sent to take of the things of Christ and show them unto you, what is the meaning of this mystery and that, and He will reveal it unto you. We have a delightful glimpse into one theological lecture-room, whose doors we would desire to set open before the eyes of every teacher and student of divinity. Fletcher of Madeley was for a while the Principal of Lady Huntingdon's training college for ministers at Trevecca in Wales. One who sat under his instructions tells us how he taught. Speaking of his sessions in the class-room, he says: " Such seasons generally terminated in this. Being convinced that to be filled with the Holy Ghost was a better qualification for the ministry than any classical learning, after speaking a while in the school-room he used to say, *'As many of you as are athirst for the fulness of the Spirit, follow me into my room.'* On this many of us have instantly followed him, and there continued for two or three

hours, wrestling like Jacob for the blessing ; and
praying one after another till we could not bear to
kneel any longer.".

We do not insist that exercises like this should
constitute the sum of all theological teaching.
Let learning have its proper place ; but we believe
that the Holy Spirit should be Head Master in every
school of divinity ; and that whatever diplomas or
degrees we may win, all are for nothing in comparison
with this one which was conferred upon the first
disciples, " *Ye have an unction from the Holy One,
and ye know all things.*"

And discovering that the Spirit of Truth is the
best instructor for the preacher, Mr. Müller con-
cluded also that he might be the best collector for
the philanthropist. Why not ? Cannot He who
openeth and no man shutteth, send His Spirit to
move the will, to unlock the coffers, and to give
the silver and the gold which are His ? That most
humiliating office of begging the Lord's money
from the Lord's people, the gracious Paraclete has
undertaken for him through long years, so that he
has lacked nothing when he has cried unto God
for hungry mouths. Oh ! to learn well this lesson
with all the rest. The shortest way to our neigh-
bour's heart is through the gates of heaven. If the
Spirit of grace and supplication rests on us, we
shall talk less to our brother to make him willing
to give, and more to God to give him the willing-
ness. We once heard Mr. Müller allude to this

crisis in his experience as the time when he determined to become " *out and out for God.*" And
how certainly when we are so, will the Holy Spirit
become out and out for us, ready to execute the
burdensome temporalities of Christian work for us ;
doing the begging of funds, and the drawing of
congregations, and the filling of pews, which the
lame faith of this generation is trying to accomplish
by fairs and festivals, by art and amusement and
sensationalism. Crutches for a limping Christianity
are all these. How quickly they would be thrown
away if the Church were truly filled with faith and
with the Holy Ghost.

And this suggests to us to consider for a little
the work which the Spirit can accomplish through
a consecrated Christian, in parish growth and exten-
sion. The history of the most conspicuous leaders
in the great Evangelical revival of the last century
in England, is singularly instructive on this point.
The experience of several of them was identical
—years of barren ministry and meagre congregations ; then in that mighty awakening, a new
anointing and illumination from the Holy Ghost,
and then crowded churches and wide-spread harvests
of souls. Not to speak of itinerants like Whitfield
and Wesley, whom we have alluded to elsewhere,
we may instance pastors of flocks like Berridge
and Venn and Walker of Truro and Grimshaw.
Where in the history of the Church can we
find the difference between a ministry of culture,

and a ministry of the Holy Ghost, so strongly marked ?

" Holy William Grimshaw " was for many years a diligent formalist, preaching the truth so far as he knew it, but with worldly aims and no personal acquaintance with the Spirit of Truth. Then came a great change, of the particulars of which we only have glimpses. But one glimpse is enough, as found in that solemn instrument of self-dedication which he drew up during this transition period. We can quote only a fragment of it :—

" Glory be to Thee, O my Triune God! Permit me to repeat and renew my covenant with Thee. I desire and resolve to be wholly and for ever Thine. Blessed God, I most solemnly surrender myself to Thee. Hear, O heaven, and give ear, O earth! I avouch this day the Lord to be my God, Father, Saviour, and portion for ever. I am one of His covenant children for ever. Record, O Eternal Lord, in Thy book of remembrance that henceforth I am Thine for ever. From this day I solemnly renounce all former lords—world, flesh, and devil—in Thy Name. No more, directly or indirectly, will I obey them. I renounced them many years ago, and I renounce them now for ever. This day I give myself up to Thee, a living sacrifice, holy and acceptable unto Thee, which I know is my reasonable service. To Thee I consecrate all my worldly possessions, in Thy service I desire and purpose to spend all my time, desiring Thee to teach me to use every moment of it to Thy glory and the setting forth of Thy praise, in every station and relation of life I am now or may hereafter be in."

This covenant, with the one of which it is a renewal, made fourteen years before, marks the first decade of his pastorate at Haworth. And what a pastorate was that! To have power to move men mightily as an evangelist is a great gift of the Spirit ; but to be the instrument of reclaiming a vast desert waste to the Lord, and making it rejoice and blossom as the rose—would that more of Christ's servants coveted this honour ; Haworth was territorially a desolate waste,—rugged, weather-beaten, and mountainous. Spiritually it was so abandoned that when Grimshaw came to it, he declared that he could ride half a day on horseback towards either point of the compass without meeting a single serious soul. But as this Spirit-baptized pastor began to preach, such power attended his ministry, that where at first he found hardly more than a score of worshippers, the church now became so crowded that many had to stand without and listen through the windows. His words were like a flame of fire, and as he preached "it was amazing to see and hear what weeping, roaring, and agony, many people were seized with at their apprehension of their sinful state and the wrath of God."

Throughout this wild region this devoted pastor went week by week, testifying of the grace of God publicly and from house to house, and warning men night and day with tears. He would often preach five times a day, rarely less than three or four, travelling forty or fifty miles to accomplish it. His spiritual communion meanwhile was so exalted that he sometimes had to ask the Lord to stay His hand, lest his mortal frame should be overpowered. From twelve communicants whom he found on coming to the parish, the number arose to twelve hundred, and this, let it be remembered, not amid a crowded city population, but in a sparsely settled country, where his hearers had often to come many miles to attend the service. Such, after a ten years' barren ministry, was the change effected when the Spirit of God came and possessed this minister of the gospel. His humility deepened meanwhile as his piety became more illustrious, so that looking on to the end he could say, " When I die, I shall then have my greatest grief and my greatest joy,—my greatest grief that I have done so little for Jesus, and my greatest joy that Jesus has done so much for me. My last words shall be, ' *Here goes an unprofitable servant.*' " Let pastors who complain of a sterile soil and a sparse and hardened population as insuperable obstacles look towards this parish of Haworth and take courage. " God is able of these stones to raise up children unto Abraham."

Would that we had space to cite other examples. We should turn our readers' eyes to Samuel Walker of Truro, England, preaching for two years with great diligence, but acting only under the inspiration, as he afterwards confessed, of two motives— " a desire of reputation and a love of pleasure "— and the result wide-spread spiritual darkness and death ; then the great change,—a ministry "not in word only but also in power, and in the Holy Ghost and in much assurance'" ; and the result, "such crowds attending his preaching that the thoroughfares of the town seemed deserted during the hours of service," while converts were numbered by the hundred yearly. Or we would point to Pastor Harms of Hermannsburg in the kingdom of Hanover. We see in the foreground a vast field beset with difficulties ; in the background a young pastor kneeling far into the night in his closet, seeking for the power of the Spirit. " I prayed fervently to the Lord ; laid the matter in His hand ; and as I rose at midnight from my knees, I said with a voice that almost startled me in the great room, *' Forward now in God's Name.'* " And after years the result is seen. From a parish ten miles square, with seven villages, but all overgrown with the tares of unbelief and formalism, a thousand at a time are seen flocking to church ; no year passes without a revival ; the number of communicants rises to eleven thousand. And the desert of 1845 is transformed into such a paradise in 1865, that it has been stated that probably no parish in Christendom equalled it in spiritual attainments, as it stood before the world in that year. What cannot the Holy Spirit accomplish if He can only find in men the " vessels unto honour, sanctified and meet for the Master's use and prepared unto every good work " ?

Let it not be thought, however, that the power of the Spirit's anointing is to be found only in such immense visible results. In the humblest service and in the lowliest sphere we observe the .same fruits. It may require as much divine boldness to speak face to face with a single sinner, as to preach to thousands. And in some who have felt themselves called of God to the service of personal conversation, we have noticed the most marked exhibitions of the Spirit's power. Time would fail us to tell of those who have been signally anointed for such work in all ages ; from Catherine of Siena in the 14th century, who used to talk with penitents all day without once stopping for food, so filled was she with the Spirit that she could say, " I have meat to eat that ye know not of," to Harlan Page and John Vassar in our own times, who won hundreds of single souls by the power of the Spirit that spoke through them.

Missionaries have by the preparation of the Spirit been " baptized into a sense of all conditions "—that hardest of all attainments to realize. Henry Martyn, at first but an indifferent Christian, writes one day in his diary, " I have resigned in profession, the riches, the honours, and the comforts of this world ; and I think also it is a resignation of the heart " ; and a little later he speaks of " *the almost supernatural fervour and deep devotion which came upon me whilst I declared that I had rightfully no other business each day but to do God's work, as a servant constantly regarding His pleasure."*

Authors have been endued with the Spirit to write for God. Ah! where is the divine baptism more vitally needed ? " *The same anointing teacheth you of all things,"* writes John. Julius Müller, with all his theological learning, seems to have needed a kind of spiritual laying on of hands, which he received from contact with the pious Tholuck, to qualify him to write his great work, " The Doctrine of Sin " ; and not less did D'Aubigné require that deeper experience and illumination referred to on another page, to fit him to produce the " History of the Reformation "—that historic. exposition of the doctrine of justification by faith. There are things of God hidden in the Scriptures, diffused through human history, and inwrought with religious experience, which no intellectual acumen, however subtle, can grasp. Therefore for every kind and quality of service we need the Paraclete. " For what man knoweth the things of a man, save the spirit of a man which is in him ? Even so the things of God knoweth no man, but the Spirit of God. Now we have received not the spirit of the world, but the Spirit which is of God ; that we might know the things that are freely given to us of God."

ACCESS AND SEPARATION.

"THE first duty is to attach oneself; detachment comes afterwards. The chrysalis covering in which the butterfly was prisoned only breaks and falls away when the insect's wings have grown—it is by opening that these burst their melancholy integuments. We only begin to detach ourselves from the world when we have learned to know something of a better. Till then we are but capable of disappointment and weariness, which are not detachment."—*Alexander Vinet.*

IX.

ACCESS AND SEPARATION.

THERE are two Advocates appointed to us, for the maintenance of our two-fold life— Christ on the throne, and the Spirit in our hearts. " If any man sin *we have an Advocate with the Father, Jesus Christ the righteous,*"* is the declaration of Scripture concerning the one ; " I will pray the Father and *He shall give you another Advocate, that He may abide with you for ever, even the Spirit of Truth,*" † is the promise of Christ concerning the other. The work of Christ for us is still going on in heaven, where " He ever liveth to make intercession." And this last saying, from the Epistle to the Hebrews, describes exactly what He is now doing for us above—viz., living for us, and interceding for us.

Does not the Scripture declare that being " reconciled to God through the death of His Son, much more being reconciled, *we shall be saved by His life*" ? ‡ This refers to His risen and glorified life. Our being is so linked with His, our salvation and

---

* 1 John ii. 1.   † John xiv. 16 (Marginal, R. V.)   ‡ Rom. v. 10.

peace are so entirely centered in His person that for Christ to live is for us to live. Hence His blessed saying, when referring to His departure out of the world, " Because I live, ye shall live also."*
And hence also that other saying of Scripture, addressed to those who are dead and risen with Christ, " *Your life is hid with Christ in God.*"
As by the death of Christ on the cross our sins were put away, our condemnation removed, and our justification perfectly accomplished, so now by the life of Christ upon the throne our spiritual growth is maintained and the work of our sanctification carried on. Meanwhile as our great High Priest within the veil, He is interceding for us ; and His intercession is but the reiteration of His atonement, a perpetual appeal to the merit of His sacrifice and death. How significant, that He who on the cross was " the Lamb of God that taketh away the sin of the world," is now " in the midst of the throne *a Lamb standing as though it had been slain.*" † Amazing words, which would tell us that the marks of His passion, the memorials of His vicarious death, are still visible on His person, and that while He intercedes for us they utter their pathetic plea to God, who is " faithful and *just* to forgive us our sins, and to cleanse us from all unrighteousness." Such is the ministry which our Advocate with the Father is continuing for us on the throne.

---

* John xiv. 19.   † Rev. v. 6, R. V.

The other Advocate is meantime perfecting His work in our hearts ; and the two ministries exactly correspond. The Comforter within is upholding and developing the inward divine life : "If Christ be in you, the body is dead because of sin, *but the Spirit is life because of righteousness.*" * He is also continuing an inward intercession according with the outward one : " *The Spirit Himself maketh intercession for us* with groanings which cannot be uttered." † Such is the double advocacy by which our two-fold life is carried on.

And observe more particularly, how each of these ministries exactly supplements the other.

The love of the Father in giving His Son to be a propitiation for our sins, is the truth which is proclaimed from every wound on our exalted Saviour's person ; and here we are to turn for the assurance of our acceptance. The moment we get taken up with our own love, as evidenced in our inward consciousness, we shall fall into darkness. God's love, as set forth in the slain Lamb upon the throne, is the only resting-place for our faith. But this is not all ; for our comfort and sanctification He also gives us His love within us, as it is written, " *Because the love of God is shed abroad in our hearts by the Holy Ghost, which is given unto us.*"‡ Again, if any challenge our justification, we turn at once and confidently to the cross where that justification was accomplished, and to the throne where it is

---

* Rom. viii. 10.   † Rom. viii. 26.   ‡ Rom. v. 5.

now maintained, and we say, " It is God that justifieth ; who is he that condemneth ? *It is Christ that died, yea rather, that is risen again, who is even at the right hand of God, who also maketh intercession for us.** But while our justification was purchased solely by Christ's death for us, our sanctification is to be effected by Christ's death in us.   And this is carried on by that other Advocate : " But if ye *through the Spirit do mortify the deeds of the body, ye shall live."* †

And yet once more, if we would be assured our of bodily resurrection, we look at once to Him whom God has raised from the dead and set at His own right hand.   If He, the First-fruits be there, we shall be there also, in a body fashioned like the body of His glory.   But this consummation also is made dependent on the inworking of the Comforter : " *If the Spirit of Him that raised up Jesus from the dead dwell in you*, He that raised up Christ from the dead shall also quicken your mortal bodies *by His Spirit that dwelleth in you."* ‡

Now Christ's presence at the Father's right hand, and His ministry in the Holy of Holies above, constitute the ground of our access there ; and this blesed fact of our privilege to enter into the Holiest by the blood of Jesus is the truth with which the Epistle to the Hebrews is especially occupied. Indeed, Christ's exaltation to the Father's throne is counted as our presence and residence there,

---

* Rom. viii. 34.   † Rom. viii. 13.   ‡ Rom. viii. 11.

and we find it so set forth in the Epistles to the Ephesians, Colossians, and Philippians. But is it not plain that access carries with it the opposite idea of separation ; that drawing near to God involves a withdrawing from fellowship with an evil world ? The fact that Christ is at the right hand of the Father, and that we are one with Him in His exaltation, gives us our reckoning-point by which to fix our relation to this world. The paradox of Lady Powerscourt that " the Christian is not one who is looking up from earth to heaven, but one who is looking down from heaven to earth," can be comprehended in this light. If " our citizenship is in heaven," * we are spiritually disfranchised of the world, and are bound to confess that " we are strangers and pilgrims on the earth." This last saying, however, is only true of believers, the " partakers of the heavenly calling." When our Lord is speaking to the unbelieving Jews, He says, " *Ye are from beneath,* I am from above ; *ye are of this world,* I am not of this world." † But when He speaks to His own disciples, to those who have been " born from above," He says, " *Ye are not of the world,* but I have chosen you out of the world." ‡ And in like manner when we read that God " hath raised us up together, and made us sit together in heavenly places in Christ Jesus," § the inference is clear concerning our earthward state. To be seated together with Christ unseats us from

---

* Phil. iii. 20.   † John viii. 23.   ‡ John xv. 19.   § Eph. ii. 6.

the throne of earthly ambition, and makes us content to forego its crowns and prizes and rewards;
just as Jesus said after speaking of the kings of the
Gentiles exercising lordship, " *but ye shall not be
so.*" This is what we mean in saying that access
implies separation.

No doubt this truth is especially distasteful to
this generation—a generation bent, as few have
been, on reconciling the claims of religion with
those of pleasure, and thus solving the problem of
" making the best of both worlds." Would that our
eyes were really open to what is passing! To dis-
suade Christians from going to the theatre would
be very tame advice in these days, when the
theatre with rapid strides is pushing itself into
the Church. To tell the disciples of Jesus to " love
not the world neither the things that are in the
world," would seem a very mild dissuasion and
almost unkind when the world has come to such
friendly terms with the Church, that it willingly
lends all its machinery of entertainment and art
and amusement to make the gospel more attractive. It is with no spirit of surly asceticism that we
speak; it is rather with a tearful, grieved, and fore-
boding dread as to where this practice of a natural-
ized Christianity and a worldly consecration may
bring us. At all events, the truest remedy is to be
found in a strenuous and stubborn non-conformity
to the world on the part of Christians. With the
most unshaken conviction, we believe that the

Church can only make headway, in this world,
by being loyal to her heavenly calling. Towards
Ritualism her cry must be "not a rag of Popery";
towards Rationalism "not a vestige of whatsoever
is not of faith"; and towards Secularism "not a
shred of the garment spotted by the flesh." The
Bride of Christ can only give a true and powerful
testimony in this world as she is found clothed
with her own proper vesture, even the "fine linen
clean and white, which is the righteousness of the
saints."

But this rigid separation from the world must
be attended with the most persistent, zealous, untir-
ing going into the world, to seek and to save that
which was lost. For the same Lord who tells us that
we are not of the world even as He is not of the world,
makes known to us how the Father sent Him into
the world, and then adds, "As my Father hath sent
me, so send I you." The other corollary of this
high doctrine—ah! who can believe it without
reserve, or receive it without shrinking—"Because ye are not of this world *therefore the world
hateth you*"? It is just as true as when Christ first
uttered it—this promise of the word's malediction
which carries the pledge of the Saviour's benediction. That we do not see this contrariety manifested, as in the beginning, is not altogether because
the world's enmity has been assuaged, but because
the Church's non-conformity has been tempered
and subdued. Settle it in your mind, oh, believer!

that if you should be privileged to walk with God like Enoch, you would have to part company with such as have set their affections on the earth ; and not content merely to walk apart from you they would have many hard speeches to make against you ; and if you should be favoured to be "greatly beloved" of the Lord, as Daniel was, your portion might be to be greatly hated by those of your generation. This we say with no morbid greed for persecution, but because it is so written. Persecution, indeed, like everything else which the Lord has blessed and sanctified, has been counterfeited by his great enemy ; and many a man who glories in tribulation is really glorying in his own shame, his fancied crown of martyrdom being only a fool's cap, which signalizes his pre-eminent self-deception. The Ritualist setting up in the Church his half-heathen ceremonials and complaining of the discipline that sets him aside from his ministry ; the Rationalist crucifying the faith of Christ with the nails of his unsanctified logic, and then, because God's true servants hold off from him, counting it persecution—What have these to do with wearing the crown of Christ's rejection ? "But if ye do well and suffer for it,"—"If any man suffer as a Christian,"—"if ye suffer for righteousness' sake, happy are ye." * And this is the promised portion of all such as will live godly in Christ Jesus. How many of us have this title and testi-

---

* 1 Peter iii. 14, etc.

mony to our consecration? Certainly, if we are faithful, it will never be wholly wanting in "this present evil world." The offence of the cross has not ceased ; and one who really lives Christ cruci-fied will be quite as likely to feel the sharp thrust of persecution, as one who preaches Christ crucified.

There was a minister of Christ, who died in the early part of this century, who exerted an extra-ordinary influence for good upon his generation, especially in awakening a spirit of self-sacrifice and consecration in other ministers. One who knew him intimately declares, and italicises the state-ment, that "*by the mere force of evangelical truth and holiness, exhibited during fifty or sixty years, and not by great talents and extraordinary powers of judgment or particular attainments in academi-cal learning,* God gave him this wide and blessed influence over the age in which he lived." * And yet we know of no one in recent times who had such a bitter portion of persecution wrung out to him, or who had such exquisite torture inflicted upon fine and tender sensibilities as this holy and evangelical preacher, Charles Simeon of Cambridge. While avoiding severity in his preaching, he poured forth from that University pulpit the tenderest and most persuasive strains of evangelical truth that could anywhere be heard in that day. Without fear, without wavering, and without qualification he preached the cross and lived the cross. But as

---

* Bishop Wilson.

he passed through the streets, he was hissed and
hooted ; bricks and stones, accompanied with every
offensive epithet, were hurled at him from college
windows, and his services in the church were constantly disturbed by angry rioters. Yet none of
these things moved him. Hear how his sorrowful
heart was once solaced in his overwhelming trials.
It is a melting story, told in his old age, and it is
most instructive in its lessons. He says : *

   " When the early disciples were persecuted and brought
before kings and governors for Christ's sake, He declared
that it should *turn to them for a testimony.* So it will be ;
the world will mock and trample on you, a man will come
and slap you on your face. You will rub your face and say,
' This is strange work, I like it not, sir '—' Never mind,' I
say. ' This is your evidence ; it turns to you for a
testimony.' If you were of the world the world would
love its own ; but now ye are not of the world, therefore
the world hateth you !
   " Many years ago when I was an object of much contempt
and derision in the University, I strolled forth one day,
buffeted and afflicted, with my little Testament in my hand.
I prayed earnestly to my God that He would comfort me
with some cordial from His word, and that, on opening the
book, I might find some texts which should sustain me. I
thought I would turn to the epistles where I should most
easily find some precious promise ; but my book was
upside down, so, without intending it, I opened on the
gospels. The first text which caught my eye was this
' *They found a man of Cyrene, Simon by name; him they compelled to bear His cross.*' You know Simon is the same name

---

* " Memoirs," p. 473.

as Simeon. What a word of instruction was here—what a blessed hint for my encouragement. To have the cross laid upon me, that I might bear it after Jesus—what a privilege ! It was enough. Now I could leap and sing for joy, as one whom Jesus was honouring with a participation in His sufferings. And when I read *that*, I said, ' Lord, lay it on me, lay it on me ; I will gladly bear the cross for Thy sake.' And I henceforth bound persecution as a wreath of glory round my brow ! "

And yet when did ever one have fellowship with Christ's sufferings, without also having part, even here, in His joy ? While the thorns of persecution were sorely wounding him, Simeon was able, like his Master, to see of the travail of his soul and be satisfied. For it was during these years of trial, that God gave him Henry Martyn, among others, as the fruit of his toil and patient endurance. Henry Martyn ! ah ! how his much sorrowing heart rested in its love when it turned to this devoted missionary ! Is there anywhere to be found a more exquisite instance of the—we will not say romance—but pathos of Christian affection, than in that story of his reception of the portrait of his beloved Henry, whose living face he was to see no more ? This is his description of the scene : " I had, after it was opened at the India House, gone to see the picture, and notwithstanding all that had been said respecting it to prepare my mind, I was so overpowered by the sight, that I could not bear to look upon it, but turned away and went to a distance, covering my face, and, in

spite of every effort to the contrary, crying aloud
with anguish. E—— was with me: and all the
bystanders said to her, 'That, I suppose, is his
father.'" *His father*, indeed, in a sense that none
of them knew; and this was the son whom he had
"begotten in his bonds." Blessed are they who,
like Simeon, are content to forego wife and children
and houses and lands for Christ's sake, that they may
look upon spiritual children and say, "for in Christ
Jesus I have begotten you through the Gospel."

We insist that the words of our Lord hold true
in all ages of the Church: "Because ye are not of
the world, therefore the world hateth you." The
power of persecution changes indeed with each
generation. In the barbarous age, it finds expression in the stake and thumbscrew; in the refined
and cultivated age it manifests itself in the form of
envenomed speech, or silent and sullen antipathy.
But whatever the form, the fact will be inevitable.
The measure of our separation from the world
must always be the measure of the world's intoler-
ance. "The age of persecution past!" Possibly,
if the age of worldly conformity is here. If the
hem of the believer's garment gets unravelled by
easy compliance, it will soon be woven up with
that of the worldling, and then there will be no
antagonism. It is the rending of garments that
uncovers deformities; drawing into closer union with
Christ results in withdrawing from the things in
which the flesh delights, and so in judging our-

selves, we condemn others. Indeed every advance
in holiness casts a reflection on prevailing worldli-
ness. Hence the enmity. " And wherefore slew
he him ? Because his own works were evil, *and
his brother's righteous.*"

We urge none to bid for persecution ; but with
the heart of Christ, we beseech Christians to strive
for unworldliness of life. " The Cross of Christ
condemns me to be a saint," wrote one. Would
that we all believed it ! Christ died that we might
live, but not unto ourselves ; He suffered that He
might reconcile us unto God,—but not unto this
present evil world.

Our power is in our separateness from the world,
not in our affiliation with it. " Why are so few,
from the world, joining the Church ? " was asked
the other day. " Because so many in the Church
are joining the world," it was answered. Explanation enough ! Nothing is gained by alliance with
unconverted men : everything depends upon our
close communion with our risen Lord. Consecration to Christ must precede contact with men, or
we shall be drawn away from Him instead of
drawing men to Him. The Holy Ghost said,
" *Separate me* Barnabas and Saul " ; and the Spirit
said to Philip, " Go near, *join thyself* to this
chariot." The first command precedes the other,
in the divine order. God would have us set
apart to Him, in order that we may with safety
and strength, go forth to bless others.

O blessed two-fold life to which He has called us ! In heaven and yet on earth ; seated with Him in the heavenlies, and sitting down with publicans and sinners to tell them of Him who died to save them ! We are as He was, who while His feet were standing on the earth, sore and weary from their search after the lost, and hastening on to be nailed to the cross for our redemption, yet spoke of Himself as the " Son of man who is *in heaven.*" Let us strive to be one with Him alike in His exaltation and in his humiliation. And to this end, let us heed that double exhortation given us in Scripture, " Let us draw near . . . having boldness to enter into the Holiest by the blood of Jesus," and " Let us go forth therefore unto Him without the camp bearing His reproach."

GRACE AND REWARD.

"O LORD, what a wonderful spirit was that which made St. Paul, in setting forth of himself against the vanity of Satan's false apostles, hand in his claim here that he in Christ's cause did excel and surpass them all? What wonderful spirit was that, I say, that made him to reckon up all his troubles and labours, his beatings, his whippings, his scourgings, his shipwrecks, his dangers and perils by water and by land, famine, hunger, nakedness, and cold, with many more, and the daily care of all the congregations of Christ, among whom every man's pain did pierce his heart, and every man's grief was grievous unto him? *O Lord, is this Paul's primacy whereof he thought so much good that he did excel all others?* Is not this Paul's saying unto Timothy, his own scholar, and doth it not pertain to whosoever will be Christ's true soldiers? Bear thou, saith he, affliction like a true soldier of Jesus Christ. This is true; if we die with Christ, we shall live with Him; if we suffer with Him, we shall reign with Him; if we deny Him, He shall deny us; if we be faithless, He remaineth faithful: He cannot deny Himself. This Paul would have known to everybody; *for there is no other way to heaven but Christ and His way.*" —BISHOP RIDLEY'S *Farewell Letter to his Fellow-Prisoners, and those who were exiled for the Gospel of Christ.*

X.

GRACE AND REWARD.

NO subject seems to be so little understood as that of divine rewards. If the Romanist has exalted merit to the utter exclusion of grace, the Protestant may be in danger of exalting grace to the utter exclusion of merit. Not that the latter has anything to do with our pardon and acceptance. As sinners standing before the mercy-seat, "there is no difference, for all have sinned and come short of the glory of God"; and therefore all must be saved on the same terms, "*being justified freely by His grace* through the redemption that is in Christ Jesus." * As saints standing before the judgment-seat, there will be a difference, since believers are to "*be judged every man according to their works.*" † Christ's work for us is the sole ground of our forgiveness; Christ's work in us will be the ground of our reward; the one is a finished work to which we can add nothing by our merit or obedience; the other is a progressive work, depending on our fidelity and consecration, whether it shall at last be crowned with the

---

* Rom. iii. 28. 29.   † Rev. xx. 13.

Master's "well done." It is evident, therefore,
that rewards have a very important place in the
scheme of redemption, and it is not necessary, in
order to magnify the grace of God, that, having
reduced all men to the same level of unworthiness,
we should fix them there for ever. What is our
Lord's promise to His faithful ones about being
" recompensed at the resurrection of the just " ?
What means the prophet's declaration, concerning
such as turn many to righteousness, that they
" shall shine as the stars for ever and ever " ?   But
it is written, " *For as one star differeth from another
star in glory,* so also is the resurrection of the
dead."   As certainly as there is no difference
between men before the cross, so certainly there
will be a difference between them in the resurrection.   Observe how clearly these two facts are
contrasted in the gospel ; grace depending solely
on the outward work of Christ on the cross, and
reward on the inward work of obedience through
the Spirit in our hearts.   Hence these two looks
enjoined in Scripture :

" *Look unto Me and be ye saved, all the ends of the
earth.*"

" *Look to yourselves, . . . that ye receive a full
reward.*" *

Now we have often noticed that just as the
legalist resents the doctrine that good works can
have no part in effecting our forgiveness, so the

---

* Isaiah xlvi. 22 ; 2 John 8 (R.V.)..

evangelical recoils from the idea that they can constitute any ground for our recompense. On the contrary, we have the feeling that such requital of faithful service and obedience is absolutely necessary to satisfy our instinctive sense of justice. We cannot think of a final divine reckoning which shall assign the same rank in glory, and the same degree of joy, to the lazy and indolent and unfruitful Christian, which are accorded to the ardent and devoted and self-denying Christian. As we cannot doubt that God, who can show Himself just and yet justify the ungodly through His faith, will at last show Himself equally just in rewarding the godly for his works. Else why lighten our possessions here except to add to our eternal weight of glory yonder? Why accept of poverty now, except to acquire "the riches of the glory of His inheritance" hereafter? As a matter of fact, when we open the Scriptures we find the discrimination between grace and reward to be clear and unvarying. Without money and without price we are saved ; with a great price must we obtain our heavenly recompense. Search the Scriptures diligently, and see how clearly this is revealed :—

"For *by grace* are ye saved through faith, *not of works*, lest any man should boast."—Eph. ii. 8, 9.

"But to him that *worketh not*, but believeth on him that justifieth the ungodly, *his faith* is counted for righteousness." — Rom. iv. 5.

"Therefore we conclude that a man is justified by

13

faith *without the deeds of law.*"—Rom. iii. 28.

"Behold I come quickly and *my reward* is with me, to give to every man *according as his work shall be.*"—Rev. xxii. 12.

"For the Son of man shall come in the glory of His Father with His angels, and then He shall *reward* every man *according to his works.*"—Matt. xvi. 27.

"Who will render to every man *according to his deeds.*"—Rom. ii. 6.

But let it be borne in mind, that while the supreme and final reward of the Christian is at the coming of Christ, the Lord has promised much even in the life that now is. The record runs, "manifold more in this present time, and in the age to come life everlasting."* The age to come is the millennial age, to be ushered in by the second advent of Christ; at which time the full reward will be meted out for losses and trials and hardships endured for Him in this age. All the crowns of the faithful are reserved unto that period;—the crown of life, the crown of joy, the crown of righteousness, the crown of glory,—all are assigned by the promise to the time of Christ's return.† Let us settle this in our minds. The present is the age of cross-bearing, wherein we are to fill up that which is behind in the sufferings of Christ; the next is the age of crown-wearing, wherein we shall fill up that which is behind in the rejoicing of Christ. For as His sufferings can never be complete while He is still afflicted in His members,

* Luke xviii. 30.
† 1 Thess. ii. 19. 2 Tim. iv. 8. 1 Peter v. 4. Rev. ii. 10.

neither can His joy be full until His Bride the
Church is with Him, beholding the glory which He
had with the Father before the world was.

Now no human biography can give us any light
concerning the rewards of that age of glory. But
the recompense of the just in this world, the
" hundredfold now in this time, *with persecutions,*"
is wonderfully illustrated in the history of Christ's
faithful servants. And to enforce this promise we
shall turn to the story of several saintly lives, and
let them tell us how much of blessed requital,
even now, the Lord bestows on those who choose
to suffer with Him.

It has often seemed as though God takes care to
reward His faithful servants most richly at the very
points where they have suffered and sacrificed
most for Him. As the clay is fashioned to the
mould, so His bounty is shaped to our privations,
His fulness to our self-emptying, His gift of Himself
to our surrender of self for His sake. Indeed is
not this the substance of what He promises in that
saying of His, " He that loseth his life for my sake
shall find it " ? He shall find the very thing, in
other words, which he has foregone, only in Christ
and not in himself; divine joy for the loss of
human happiness, spiritual riches for the spoiling
of earthly goods, favour with the Lord's people for
the enmity and rejection of the world. Surely we
may comfort ourselves unspeakably in this fact, in
the face of any trial or hardship which we may

be moved to undergo for the Master's sake. He
never leaves Himself without this witness to His
tender love and gracious care of His own. His
reward will always take its measure from our privation ; and if we can say truly, " Behold we have
left all and followed thee," we shall certainly have
the promise fulfilled to us, " All things are yours,
and ye are Christ's, and Christ is God's." As
much of self-sacrifice, so much of the divine indwelling is the law of the Spirit of life, even as every
indenture of the coast means a corresponding fulness of the incoming tide. Therefore we need not
think it strange that the same apostle who had
"suffered the loss of all things " for Christ, could
yet speak of himself as " possessing all things."

This is the lesson most deeply impressed upon
us from the life of that rare Christian of the last
century, Gerhard Tersteegen of Mulheim in Germany. Born in 1697 ; begotten again at sixteen
years of age ; soon after so wrought upon by the
Spirit that he often spent whole nights in prayer
and supplication ; then his renunciation of wealth
and comfort, that with all his substance he might
minister to the poor ; then his noble dedication of
himself to God in written covenant ; and then the
years of obloquy and desertion by formal Christians.—This, in brief, is the story of his life.
But in the midst of it all what immeasurable
compensations ! No thought of making himself
attractive or widely influential seems to have

entered his mind. But just when he was most
shunned and deserted by the worldly, then the sin-
burdened and sorrowing began to crowd upon him
from every direction, to crave his spiritual ministrations. Mark it well, oh popular preacher, com-
passing all art and originality in order to draw the
people! Here was one who had no thought of
drawing anybody, his heart being set only on the
one end of becoming holy unto the Lord, and perfectly doing His will. Indeed, while pursuing his
humble calling as a ribbon maker, how little he
anticipated being a preacher at all. But like his
Master, for Whom he lived supremely, "he could
not be hid." The people thronged upon him.
He tried to withdraw from them, but so much the
more they pressed about him. Before he had risen
in the morning, fifty or sixty would gather at his
lodgings to hear the word of life from his lips;
while state-church clergymen were jealous of his
irregular ministry, and complaining of him to the
magistrates, he was yielding to the importunity of
hungry souls, and consenting to preach; and such
crowds gathered that they not only filled every
part of the house, but climbed on ladders about
the windows, in their eagerness to catch his words.
One totally unknown to him comes two hundred
miles on foot and in bad weather that he may
hear the words of this blessed man. But Tersteegen meantime is strangely amazed at it all,
since his discourse is so plain and so unstudied. " I

cannot think what the people seek from such a
poor creature," he exclaims.   Yet the secret is
clear to us who read his life to-day.   Give thyself
wholly to Christ, and Christ will give Himself
wholly to thee ; all the infinite wealth of His temporal and spiritual favour freely bestowed.   "*Jesus
alone is sufficient,*" he wrote, "*yet insufficient when
He is not wholly and solely embraced.*"   True without question is the saying, and equally true that
those who wholly embrace Him shall have " all-
sufficiency in all things, and abound unto every
good work."   Think of this good man, once shunned
and derided as a fanatic, now pressed upon by
such eager crowds of anxious souls, that he can
hardly find time to eat or sleep ; once lying alone
in an attic, burning up with fever, and so poor and
neglected that from morning till night no one
brought him even a cup of water, now made the
recipient of such sumptuous legacies from friends
whom he had never seen, and from spiritual kinsmen
in foreign lands, that he feels obliged to decline
them.   How was he enriched unto all bountiful-
ness, temporal and spiritual, even as he heartily
and without reserve embraced what he calls " *the
mystery of the inward and the outward cross.*"   Can
we wonder that he should have given this as his
estimate of life ?

"Methinks it would be an inexpressible consolation to
me, if in my dying hour, and when I shall have to appear in
the presence of God, I could proclaim to all the world that

God alone is the fountain of life, and *that there is no other way to find and enjoy Him than the narrow way of inward prayer, self-denial, and a life hid with Christ in God, opened out to us and consecrated by the death of the Saviour.*"

And unconscious, far-reaching spiritual attractiveness was the special reward of self-denial which he reaped. It is an honourable ambition to crave the power of drawing men, if we are intent only on bringing them to Christ. But let us remember that the true centre of gravitation is the cross. "I if I be lifted up will draw *all men unto me.*" Whether by word or by example, whether by the preaching in which Jesus Christ is "evidently set forth crucified," or by the life in which His cross and obedience unto death shine out conspicuously, this is the strongest attraction. Oh to learn this lesson well, that through our self-renunciation, God's drawing power is most effectively brought to bear on human souls. Gerhard Terstegeen carried his renunciation so far as to be willing to forego the joy of divine communion if it must be. In seasons of spiritual abandonment and barrenness, he advised that we neither turn to the world for comfort nor persist in begging of God that comfort which He, for the time, is pleased to withhold. He says :—

"Before the day of Pentecost arrived, the disciples could not hold out long in solitude, without the bodily and visible presence of Jesus. 'I go a fishing,' said Peter. Time appeared long to them in solitude; and such is the case with us. We go, as it were, a fishing, in a book, in company with others, etc. ; and it is a favour if, having caught nothing during the night, the Saviour meets us and shows us, as He did the disciples, the fruitlessness of all such attempts. I testify with fear, shame, and deep acknowledgment of the divine long-suffering and goodness, what my own experience has taught me in this respect; that the exercise of prayer is of so much importance, and that in seasons of inward darkness and barrenness, we fall into the temptation so easily. But, on the other hand, when we cannot proceed with the exercise of prayer in the customary manner, we ought not to hold fast with firm efforts and self-will what the Lord pleases to take from us; but humble ourselves, quietly consent to our nakedness and poverty, sacrifice our relish, light, and pleasure to His good pleasure, and make the latter our prayer and our food; we should thus find, in time, the advantage of letting go of ourselves, of privation, and the loss of self, so to speak, and be made capable of a more profound, or rather of a purer retirement, made of prayer, and union with God, which is the very object the Lord has in view." *

What a depth of self-abnegation is here reached ! To accept the cross of withheld communion, the self-denial of the divine favour, for the sake of the deeper humiliation and chastening—this is to go far beyond the common bounds of obedience. And we cannot wonder that the recompense attending it so far transcended the ordinary limits ; so that from sharing his Master's trial of being despised and rejected of men, he shared also his Master's glory, and unto him was the gathering of the people.

* "Life and Letters," pp. 169, 170.

We are speaking thus far of the present return which the Lord makes for faithful service. Sometimes this comes after the death of the servant of God ; it is in the time that now is, but after the departure of him who has earned it. This seems to be the promise in the beatitude of the faithful dead given in the Apocalypse ; " for they rest from their labours ; *and their works do follow them.*" *

Their hands have ceased from toil and their tongue is silent ; but because their labour was so truly in the Lord it continues in perpetual increase and blessing on the earth. They did not live to behold the fruit of their service ; but the generations following see it and praise their memory.

Let us stand for a moment at the grave of one of these blessed ones who died in the Lord. It is in St. Mary's chancel in Taunton, England. We stoop down and read the inscription :—" Here lies Master Joseph Alleine of Taunton—a sacrifice to God and to you " ;—and our thoughts run back to that November day in 1668 when this grave was closed. There stands the widowed Theodosia, the partner of his sorrows, and the mourner for his early death. Beside her is the aged George Newton, his beloved brother and companion in tribulation ; and close by John Howe with a weeping train who have come over from a neighbouring parish to look for the last time upon the face of

---

* Rev. xiv. 13.

this endeared servant of Christ.* What thoughts must fill their minds as they try to justify the ways of God to men? This faithful minister, so gifted by nature, so unreservedly devoted to God, brought to his grave at the age of thirty-five, utterly broken by long imprisonment and heartless persecution, his candle put out when darkness is covering the land and gross darkness the people, and he such a burning and shining light,—how could the Lord permit it? If such thoughts arise in the heart of the widowed one, let her turn back to that beautiful letter written to her in the early days of their espousal. Did Joseph Alleine have a presentiment of the sorrowful future that lay before them? Did the shadows of Ilchester prison already stretch across his path? It would almost seem so. But let us read from the letter :—

"None ever was, or ever shall be, a loser by Jesus Christ. Many have lost much *for* Him, but never did, never shall any lose *by* Him. Take this for a certainty, whatsoever probabilities of outward comforts we leave, whatsoever outward advantages we balk, that we may glorify Him in our services, and enjoy Him in His ordinances more than others where we could, we shall receive an hundredfold in this life. 'Tis a sad thing to see how little Christ is trusted or believed in the world; men will trust Him no farther than they can see Him, and will leave no work for faith. Hath He not a thousand ways, both outward and inward, to make up a little outward dis-

---

* "Joseph Alleine: His Companions and Times," by Chas. Stanford. London : Hodder & Stoughton.

advantage to us ? What doth our faith serve for ? Have any ventured themselves upon Him in His way, but He made good every word of the promise to them ? Let us therefore exercise our faith, and stay ourselves upon the promise, and see if ever we are ashamed of our hope.

"What is wanting in the means, God will make up in the blessing. This I take for a certain truth, while a man commits himself and his affairs to God, and is in a way that God put him into : now if a man have but a little income, if he have a great blessing, that's enough to make it up. We must not account mercies by the bulk. What if another have a pound to my ounce ? If mine be gold for his silver, I will never change with him. As 'tis not bread that keeps men alive, but the word of blessing that proceedeth out of the mouth of God; so 'tis not the largeness of the means, but the blessing of the Lord that maketh rich. Oh ! if men did but believe this, they would not grasp as much of the world as they do. Well, let others take their course, and we will take ours, to wait upon God by faith and prayer, and rest in His promise; and I am confident that is the way to be provided for."

All this was truly prophetic : " *Hath He not a thousand ways, both outward and inward, to make up a little outward disadvantage to us ?* " We shall see what some of these ways were in his case. But let us first glance for a moment at the man. Such a life of prayer he lived, that he carried the very atmosphere of heaven about with him. Neither prison damps nor the corrupt manners of his age could vitiate this atmosphere. "All his garments smelled of myrrh and aloes and cassia," as one who daily walked with God in

Paradise. "At the time of his health," writes
his beloved wife, "he did rise constantly at or
before four of the clock; and would be much
troubled if he heard smiths or other craftsmen at
work at their trades before he was at communion
with God; saying to me often, 'How this noise
shames me! Doth not my Master deserve more
than theirs?' From four till eight he spent in
prayer, holy contemplation and singing of psalms,
in which he much delighted and did daily practise
alone or with his family." Here are laid bare the
sources of that cheerful heavenly mindedness
which so powerfully impressed those with whom
he came in contact. And his preaching was perfectly mated to his praying. "He was infinitely
and insatiably greedy for the conversion of souls,
wherein he had no small success in the time of his
ministry; and to this end he poured out his very
heart in prayer and in preaching: he imparted not
the Gospel only, but his own soul. His supplications and his exhortations many times were so
affectionate, so full of holy zeal, life, and vigour,
that they quite overcame his hearers; he melted
over them, so that he thawed and mollified and
sometimes dissolved the hardest hearts."

All the story of his imprisonment for conscience'
sake, his trial of cruel mockings and revilings, all
the ungodly deeds which the ungodly committed
against him, and all the hard speeches which ungodly sinners spoke against him—these things we

must pass over. Only let us know of his patient endurance, of his unretaliating silence under misrepresentation, and yet of his stern refusal to be silent anywhere, and at any time, when he could preach the Gospel to perishing souls ; only let us hear what was his joy and hope and unfailing consolation amid all his trials. Here is a brief passage from one of his letters :—

"Verily, sir, it is but a little while that prisons shall hold us. Surely He is gone to prepare a place for us ; and He will come again to receive us to Himself, that where He is we may be also. And what have we to do but to believe, and wait and love, and long and look out for His coming, in which is all our hope. 'Twill be time enough for us to be preferred then. We know beforehand who shall then be uppermost." *

But Alleine's recompense was not altogether deferred to the time of Christ's coming. Have we noticed that significant promise concerning the suffering Messiah—" *He shall prolong His days*" ?† He was " cut off out of the land of the living " ; His days on the earth prematurely ended ; but they

---

* It is good to hear such a true note struck concerning the Christian's hope and reward. No talk of that sentimental heaven fitted up with modern improvements, which is so popular in our times ! In another place, speaking of the death of his father, he says : " But I bless the Lord I do believe and expect the return of the Redeemer with all His saints, and the most glorious resurrection of my own dead body with all believers ; and this makes me rest in hope, and fills me with unspeakably more joy than the death of myself or any other saint can with grief."

† Isa. liii. 10.

were prolonged in the ministry of the Spirit and
in the lives of His followers. And what was true
of Him, is true in a measure of His faithful servants
in all ages. Joseph Alleine was cut off at thirty-
five years of age, only one-half of man's allotted
time upon the earth being given him. But he left
behind him, among other writings, one brief treatise, called " The Alarm to the Unconverted." It
is a plain book, endowed with none of those
elements of a literary immortality which belong to
the famous works of his brother Puritans—having
nothing of the glowing imagery of Bunyan's " Pilgrim's Progress," or of the sparkling brilliance of
Gurnall's " Christian Armour." But thirty-five years
after the author's death Dr. Calamy wrote : " No
book in the English tongue, the Bible only ex-
cepted, can equal it for the number that hath been
dispersed." Men would call its career a literary
marvel, thirty thousand copies being once struck
off at a single edition, so great was the demand.
We call it a divine and visible seal affixed by the
Lord to the fidelity of one of His anointed ones.
It would seem as though God breathed into it a
special inspiration of His Spirit, saying, " Since
wicked men have cut off my well-beloved servant
by their persecutions, so that he lived out but half
his days on the earth, I decree him to live on after
his death, to prolong his days and see his seed, in
the influence of this little book." It is altogether
unprecedented, so far as our knowledge goes—

this *post-mortem* ministry of the best of Puritans. We hear of an indolent Scotch minister reading parts of this book to his congregation, and a revival resulting therefrom, which swept over a whole region with its transforming power. Oh, wise and trusting servant of God, serenely suffering in the kingdom and patience of Jesus Christ, and enduring "as seeing him that is invisible," how true thy words, "*Hath he not a thousand ways, both outward and inward, to make up a little outward disadvantage to us ?*" He who loved the preaching of the Gospel and the saving of souls better than his own life, wrought, by this work, even more mightily after his death than by his oral teaching in his life.

God is not limited to present times and circumstances in giving His servants the reward of their labour. The shutting of one pulpit may be but the opening of a wide and effectual door into another. Edwards in New England, Spener in Germany, Monod in France, were each thrust out of their churches, and their places of testimony closed against them, because they moved for a purer faith and a higher style of Christian living than that prevailing about them. But no smallest loss of influence or usefulness was thereby incurred.

And then there is the inner joy, the testimony of a good conscience in the breast of those who have been faithful unto death in their witness for Christ. Here is a spiritual revenue, over and

above all others. "God pays, but not always at
the end of the week," says an oft-quoted proverb ;
and we may add, nor always in the same currency.
By a divine exchange He often settles temporal
losses with spiritual coin, a coin which bears only
the image and superscription of Christ, and
therefore has no value in the world's markets, but
which is of inestimable worth to such as have
spiritual discernment. How endless the illustrations of this inward spiritual requital if we had
space to consider them. Here is the patience
and faith of the saints — the balm of the Spirit
healing the wounds of the sword, the reality of
heavenly citizenship assuaging all the pains and
privations of earthly exile.

We need not wonder if Zinzendorf, who exclaims from a glowing heart, " I have one passion ;
it is He, He alone," should soon find himself the
object of bitterest contempt in a world whose one
passion is self and self alone. But what matters
it ? "By faith Noah . . . prepared an ark to the
saving of his house, *by which he condemned the
world.*" A holy choice of God and life eternal as
our supreme good will cast an inevitable reflection
upon such as mind earthly things. But the portion of such is with the Lord, and in the communion that lifts us into his presence. Slander and
detraction followed Zinzendorf as dark shadows
follow a brilliant light. He who had renounced
earthly citizenship, owning that " that place is our

proper home where we have the greatest oppor-
tunity of labouring for our Saviour," found his
residence for years in exile. But in the midst of it
all he could say, "I would rather be despised and
hated for the sake of Jesus than be beloved for
my own sake." Weighed down with labour, and
often bearing the heavy cross of obloquy, he could
yet exclaim concerning a journey, "*All the way I
swam in peace and joy in the Lord.*"

Thrice blessed are they who have such a portion.
"And your joy no man taketh from you," says the
Saviour. Let God's servants be incited, by these
brief glimpses of suffering and victorious lives, to
choose this divine inheritance. "It is a faithful
saying : For if we be dead with Him, we shall also
live with Him ; if we suffer with Him, we shall
also reign with Him ; if we deny Him, He also
will deny us ; if we believe not, yet He abideth
faithful, He cannot deny Himself."

14

"HUMAN wisdom says, 'Disengage yourself by degrees from the bonds of sin; learn gradually to love God and live for Him.' But in this way we never break radically with sin, and give ourselves wholly to God. We remain in the dull, troubled atmosphere of our own nature, and never attain to the contemplation of the full light of the Divine holiness. Faith, on the contrary, raises us, as it were at a bound, into the regal position which Jesus Christ now holds, and which in Him is really ours. From thence we behold sin cast under our feet; we taste the life of God as our true essential being in Jesus Christ. Reason says, '*Become* holy in order to *be* holy.' Faith says 'You *are* holy: therefore become so. You are holy in Christ; become so in your own person.' This is perhaps the most paradoxical feature of pure evangelical doctrine. He who disowns it, or puts it from him, will never cross the threshold of Christian sanctification. We do not get rid of sin by little and little, we break with it with that total breaking which was consummated by Christ upon the cross. We do not ascend one by one the steps of the throne: we spring upon it and seat ourselves there with Christ by the act of faith which incorporates us in Him. Then from the height of that position, holy in its essential nature, we reign victoriously over self, the world, Satan, and all the powers of evil."—*Godet.*

XI.

IDEAL AND ATTAINMENT.

CONCLUSION.

WHAT we have thus set forth from Scripture and experience we would wish to see
made real in Christian life. But we are sensible
that to live a truth is far more difficult than to
expound it. And yet it is to be borne in mind
that doctrine is not the measure of experience,
but its mould. For example, instead of aiming at
self-crucifixion as the goal of our endeavour, we
start from it as our point of departure. "*I have
been crucified with Christ,*" * writes Paul. Here is
the doctrinal or judicial fact on which he rests
and from which he proceeds. And how constantly
is he reiterating it as a truth applying to all
believers without distinction. "Because we thus
judge that one died for all, *therefore all died.*" †
And what is his conclusion from this solemn
judicial fact? This, that we are to strive with all
diligence to make it a realized and experimental
fact. "For ye died, . . . *mortify therefore your*

---

* Gal. ii. 20 (R. V.).   † 2 Cor. v. 15 (R. V.).

members which are upon the earth." * That is to
say, we are to make that true in ourselves which
is already true for us in Christ, and so turn a fact
of doctrine into a fact of attainment. And this
principle applies to resurrection equally. "*Raised
together with Christ*," we are to "*seek those things
that are above*" ; † that is, to live the resurrection
life in Him instead of holding to the fallen life in
Adam.

Now it is already true that the Holy Ghost has
been given ; therefore we are to receive Him in
His indwelling fulness and power. It is true that
all believers are sanctified, for Paul addresses the
Corinthian church in its entirety as "*those that
are sanctified in Christ Jesus*" ; therefore are we
to seek with all diligence to be sanctified in ourselves, that our whole soul, body, and spirit may be
presented blameless before the Lord at His coming.
Here, readers, is what we mean by the "two-fold
life." It is Christ's work for us, on the cross, on
the throne, and in the clouds, on the one hand ;
and Christ's work in us, by His Spirit, by His
Word, and by His ordinances on the other. And
the high endeavour, the life-long task which is set
before us in the Scriptures, is that of conforming
our inward experience to our outward standard, or in
the expressive words of Paul, " Of apprehending that
for which we are also apprehended of Christ
Jesus." With us, Christian attainment is not a

---

* Col. iii. 3 (R. V.).   † Col. iii. 1.

tentative, uncertain thing. God does not say to each one of us, " Be what you can be ; and since each man is architect of his own fortune, reach forth to the end for which you are best fitted." Nay ; God never talks to us, as men do, about being the architects of our own fortunes ; but He holds up before us that archetype of our spiritual fortune which He has fashioned for us, and declares that this must so certainly be wrought out in us that He counts it done already, saying, " For whom He did foreknow He also did predestinate to be conformed to the image of His Son. Moreover, whom He did predestinate them He also called ; and whom He called them He also justified ; and whom He justified them He also glorified." *

It should be an occasion of sincere gratitude, we believe, that the great evangelistic movement now going on is emphasizing so strongly the doctrine that justification and assurance rest on the external work and the external word of Christ. Inquirers are told to look for the evidence of their salvation to what the Redeemer has done for them on His Cross, and to what He has said to them in His Testament, and not to what they can discover going on within their hearts. This is the true doctrine of justification by faith which it was the work of the Reformation to revive. Faith never draws attention to itself, but points ever to the finished work of Christ. " Therefore being justified

* Rom. viii. 30.

by faith."—But the "*therefore*" carries the thought back to the preceding verse, and throws the whole weight of our confidence on the accomplished fact therein stated ; * "Who was delivered for our offences and raised again for our justification."

The Wesleyan revival of a hundred years ago laid weighty emphasis on the doctrine of the inward witness. This was necessary and inevitable in a movement which reacted so strongly from the barren Externalism then prevailing in the Church. But we have the impression that in the course of time this emphasis became excessive and oppressive, and tended to put upon anxious souls a burden greater than they could bear. How many of us remember in our own conversion the persistency with which our gaze was directed within, and how painfully we were set to watch our spiritual exercises to find the evidences of our acceptance. But now the pendulum has swung quite to the opposite extreme, and our most effective revival preachers disparage all trust in frames and feelings, telling sinners to look to Christ on the Cross, instead of searching for Christ in the heart ; to receive the testimony of the Word to their acceptance, when they have believed, instead of searching for the testimony of consciousness. This we strongly believe to be the true gospel. And there

---

* "Look to the wounds of Christ, brother Martin, look to the wounds of Christ, and there you will see how God feels toward you."— *Staupitz to Luther.*

is so much the more need of giving the other phase of doctrine its true place, in order to preserve the balance of truth. We should urge the seeking of the witness of the Spirit, not as the ground of faith, but as the fruit of faith. Paul has given us the two-fold life in a single paragraph in the Epistle to the Galatians—" For ye are all sons of God *by faith in Christ Jesus.*" "And *because* ye are sons, God hath sent forth the Spirit of His Son into your hearts, crying, Abba, Father."*

It seems to us that the old Puritan writers held together these two sides of truth, and preserved their balance to a remarkable degree. They expounded most clearly the objective work of Christ, and they also unfolded His subjective work, with a minuteness and a depth of insight quite beyond anything we witness in our day. And they wrote thus clearly because they had apprehended these things by a profound interior experience. What tide-marks do the diaries and meditations which these good men left, furnish of the heights to which the Spirit's floods rose in their souls! We have a great lesson to learn of them concerning the culture of the inner life.

Reading the high discourse of John Howe on " The Blessedness of the Righteous," " Delighting in God," and " The Redeemer's Tears," we instinctively inquire for the spiritual autobiography of this man who writes so divinely. We are dis-

* Gal. iii. 26 ; iv. 6.

appointed, however, to find that he ordered all his
journals to be burned before his death, and that in
spite of the remonstrance of friends these were committed to the flames.   But he has more than once
expressed his sense of the importance of striving
for the highest communion and delight in God
which the soul may attain through the Holy Ghost.
And there is one glimpse into his inner experience
which shows how clearly he apprehended the two-
fold life.   On the blank page of his Bible, penned
in Latin, we find this record :—

December 26th, 1689.

" After that I had long, seriously, and repeatedly thought
with myself, *that besides a full and undoubted assent to the
objects of faith, a vivifying, savoury taste and relish of them
was also necessary, that with stronger force and more powerful energy they might penetrate into the most inward centre of
my heart, and there being most deeply fixed and rooted, govern
my life;* and that there could be no other sure ground
whereon to conclude and pass a sound judgment, on my
good estate Godward ; and after I had in my course of
preaching been largely insisting on 1 Cor. i. 12.   For our
rejoicing is this, the testimony of our conscience, etc. ; this
very morning I awoke out of a most ravishing and delightful dream, when a wonderful and copious stream of celestial
rays, from the lofty throne of the Divine Majesty, did seem
to dart into my open and expanded breast.   I have often
since with great complacency reflected on that very signal
pledge of special Divine favour vouchsafed to me on that
noted, memorable day; and have with repeated fresh
pleasure tasted the delights thereof.   But what of the same
kind I sensibly felt, through the admirable bounty of my God,

and the most pleasant comforting influences of the Holy
Spirit, on October 22nd, 1704,* far surpassed the most expressive words my thoughts can suggest. I then experienced
an inexpressibly pleasant melting of heart, tears gushing out
of mine eyes, for joy that God should shed abroad His love
abundantly through the hearts of men, and that for this
very purpose mine own should be so signally possessed of
and by His blessed Spirit. Romans. v. 5."

Rightly does this lofty thinker hold that it is
the divine life within, penetrating to the most
inward centre, and being deeply fixed and rooted
there, which determines our character. The outward look of faith saves us ; the inward life of
faith sanctifies us. The human face takes its
expression from the soul within, that inner sculptor who fashions our features by the touch of
thought and feeling and desire. No countenance
can *copy* the lines of beauty or grace from another ;
they must be shaped from within. And so it is
" the law of the Spirit of Life " operating within
us that determines our character and example, not
any external imitation. The Apostle says, indeed,
that " we all with open face beholding as in a glass
the glory of the Lord, are changed into the same

* This reference is probably to an experience thus described by his
biographer. " It was observed, and is, I believe, to this day remembered
by some of his flock, that in his last illness, and when he had been
declining for some time, he was once in a most affecting, melting
heavenly frame at the communion, and carried out into such a ravishing
and transporting celebration of the love of Christ, that both he himself
and they who communicated with him were apprehensive he would
have expired in that very service."

image from glory to glory." But this transformation is not effected by outward conformity, but
through an inner moulding. For he adds, " *Even
by the Spirit of the Lord.*" Can we, then, attach
too much importance to the indwelling and inworking of the Comforter ?

And this leads us to recur again to the question
of the enduement and inhabiting of the Holy
Spirit. ˙ Mark how all power, success, knowledge,
and conviction are made in the Scriptures to
depend on this. Nothing of eloquence or learning
is ˙ mentioned in the descriptions of primitive
preaching. But the record is that they "preached
the Gospel unto you *with the Holy Ghost sent down
from heaven.*" * No powerful array of logic is
recommended for convincing an unbelieving world
of the deity of the Christ. On the contrary, we are
admonished that "no man can say that Jesus is
Lord *but by the Holy Ghost.*" † No fixed and
accredited prayers are provided for the ignorant
and stammering ; but the declaration is explicit
that "we know not what we should pray for as we
ought, but *the Spirit Himself maketh intercession
for us with groanings which cannot be uttered.*"‡
No intimation is given that Christians are to borrow
the world's pleasures for their comfort and delec-
tation in their earthly pilgrimage ; but the picture
of their state is that of believers " *walking in the
comfort of the Holy Ghost.*"§ If so much is made

---

* 1 Peter i. 12.　† 1 Cor. xii. 3.　‡ Rom. viii. 26.　§ Acts ix. 31.

to depend on the indwelling Spirit, how diligently we need to seek the largest measure and the fullest communication of His power, which are possible for us.

We do not insist that it is God's will that all shall have the same overpowering baptism of the Spirit which Finney and Brainerd Taylor had ; or be visited with such seraphic delights as Edwards and Howe and Flavel enjoyed, or be favoured with such times of refreshing as were vouchsafed to Brainerd and Christmas Evans. But the anointing of the Spirit to fit us for the highest service and success—this seems to be something for which all may rightly seek. And how may it be obtained ? for this is the question we are called to answer in this chapter.

1. By prayer, continued, definite, and persevering, we answer first of all. As we become deeply instructed in this matter, we shall learn to pray less about the details of duty, and more about the fulness of power. The manufacturer is chiefly anxious to secure an ample head of water for his mills ; and this being found, he knows that his ten thousand spindles will keep in motion without particular attention to each one. It is in like manner the sources of our power that we should be most solicitous about, and not its results. If by real prayer we have gained access to God and obtained the communication of the Spirit, every service will be quickened, every duty will be in-

spired, every infirmity will be helped. Let us pray, therefore, with all perseverance for the Holy Spirit, watching thereunto, until through faith and patience we inherit the promise. We have said that our Master's sealing was the pattern for ours. And have we observed how it came to Him while in intercession to His Father? " Jesus also having been baptized *and praying*, the heaven was opened and the Holy Ghost descended in a bodily form as a dove upon Him," *—suggesting that even the Son of God did not receive this gift without asking for it. Continue therefore in supplication, O believer, for this greatest of blessings. All gifts are wrapped up in the gift of the Spirit, all powers are included in the power of the Holy Ghost. Give not over asking till you are answered, and the Lord shall once more say to you, " Receive ye the Holy Ghost."

2. By a diligent study of the Holy Scriptures we shall most assuredly be in the way of attaining this blessing. " *The Spirit of God rides most triumphantly in His own chariot,*"† says a worthy Puritan. And we know from repeated declarations that the word of God is the vehicle of the Spirit. " Sanctify them through Thy truth," prays Jesus ; " Thy Word is truth." If we mount up to God in the chariot of faith and intercession, we may look for Him to come down to us in the chariot of truth. Let us therefore search the

* Luke iii. 22 (R. V.).   † Thomas Manton, 1620—1677.

Scriptures diligently to discover what treasures of the Spirit are there hidden for us.

3. By association with those servants of God who have most of the Spirit's life in their souls we may find this grace. The instances in the Acts of the Apostles of believers sent to communicate the Spirit to those who had Him not are suggestive. Without arguing that there are those who can bestow this gift in the same way to-day, the method is significant of God's general order. He has put this treasure into earthen vessels that it may the more readily be poured into others of the same kind. And often these vessels are very humble and little esteemed among men ;—hidden Christians who are intimate with God ; lowly women of whom the world is not worthy ; followers with some despised sect, or dwellers in some illustrious obscurity—these are they who have often proved God's very chiefest instruments for leading Christians into the fuller power and larger light of the Spirit.

It is more than interesting, it is altogether humbling and subduing, to trace instances of this sort. There is John Tauler, the splendid preacher and theologian, at fifty years of age quite without a peer among his contemporaries. What higher accomplishments, what added power does he need ? But a mysterious stranger comes to Strasburg in 1340—Nicolas of Basle, a leader in the sect of "Friends of God." He gets the ear of this man who has the ear of all the people, and shows him

that it is not by might of learning or splendour of
eloquence, but by God's Spirit, that he is to fulfil
his ministry. And the admired preacher at length
leaves his pulpit for two whole years to seek in
retirement that spiritual enduement to which he
had hitherto been a stranger. And how he
preached when he emerged from his solitude and
again ascended the pulpit! What searching intensity
of speech, what profound humility, what Christ-like
compassion for the sins and sorrows of his people ;
what apostolic self-denial ! Living in an age which
has been named " an epoch of tears, of blood, of
unmeasured calamity," he was such a prophet and
apostle of God as few succeeding ages have known.

There is Francis Xavier, in the sixteenth century. He has early risen into brilliant reputation ;
and crowds are thronging his lectures day by day.
Who has achieved success if he has not ? But
in the throng of his hearers appears the sombre
figure of Ignatius Loyola. Disliked, ridiculed,
repulsed at first, he does not leave the object of
his solicitude ; but after each splendid success he
plies him with the question, " What shall it profit
a man if he gain the whole world and lose his own
soul ? " At last, under this searching inquisition,
Xavier is driven into retirement, and his ambitious
thoughts are remanded to the cloister of his peni-
tent heart, there to be trained into obedience to the
cross of Christ. When he comes forth he is girded
for service. Oh that he had known the true gos-

pel of the grace of God—this missionary of un-
equalled fortitude, this undaunted cross-bearer, who
became obedient unto death for his Master's sake !
But for becoming what he was he owed the first
impulse to that stern-visaged Spaniard. These are
but illustrations, which might be greatly multiplied, of the power of single men in leading their
fellows to a higher life. The lesson is a very practical and serious one. It may be that through
some very lowly instrument shall come to us the
greatest blessing of our life. "The secret of the
Lord is with them that fear Him"; and on this
principle it often happens that they are best
instructed in the things of God who are least
instructed in the things of men, and that the highest
divine wisdom is found with those of lowliest human
station. See that ye despise not one of these little ones,
for they may have been commissioned of the Lord
to bear to you one of His most precious secrets.

We select an example which is found near home
and which belongs to a very practical and powerful ministry. No one at all acquainted with our
eminent American Evangelist can question his
superior natural endowments ; his intense sympathy, his sturdy Saxon common sense, and his great
executive talent. But, on the other hand, no one
acquainted with his work can believe that these
qualities alone can account for his remarkable
success. Mr. Moody believes intensely in the

enduement of the Holy Spirit as the source of
the preacher's power ; and those who have followed
him in his extraordinary work will be sure that he
has known something of this in his own experience. From an address given recently in Glasgow
we get a glimpse of his spiritual history, which
accords remarkably with what we have just been
saying. We give it in his own words, as found in
a published report of his sermons :—

"I can myself go back almost twelve years and remember
two holy women who used to come to my meetings. It
was delightful to see them there, for when I began to
preach I could tell by the expression of their faces they
were praying for me. At the close of the Sabbath evening
services they would say to me, 'We have been praying
for you.' I said, 'Why don't you pray for the people?'
They answered, '*You* need power.' 'I need power,' I said
to myself; 'why, I thought I had power.' I had a large
Sabbath school, and the largest congregation in Chicago.
There were *some* conversions at the time, and I was in a
sense satisfied. But right along these two godly women
kept praying for me, and their earnest talk about 'the
anointing for special service' set me thinking. I asked
them to come and talk with me, and we got down on our
knees. They poured out their hearts, that I might receive
the anointing of the Holy Ghost. And there came a great
hunger into my soul. I knew not what it was. I began to
cry as never before. The hunger increased. I really felt
that I did not want to live any longer if I could not have
this power for service. I kept on crying all the time that
God would fill me with His Spirit. Well, one day, in the
city of New York—oh, what a day !—I cannot describe it ; I
seldom refer to it ; it is almost too sacred an experience to
name. Paul had an experience of which he never spoke

for fourteen years. I can only say, God revealed Himself to me, and I had such an experience of His love that I had to ask Him to stay His hand.

" I went to preaching again. The sermons were not different; I did not present any new truths, and yet hundreds were converted. I would not be placed back where I was before that blessed experience if you would give me all Glasgow. It is a sad day when the convert goes into the Church and that is the last you hear of him. If, however, you want this power for some selfish end, as, for example, to gratify your ambition, you will not get it. 'No flesh, says God, shall glory in my presence.' May He empty us of self and fill us with His presence."

This is a story often repeated in the history of God's Church—humble instruments used to prepare the mightiest instruments for their work. How obscure a figure is Ananias in comparison with Paul! And yet he is the one commissioned to communicate the Spirit to this chief apostle, that this " chosen vessel " who is to bear Christ's name to the Gentiles may first " be filled with the Holy Ghost." How slight the mention made in Scripture of Aquila and Priscilla! But these are they who took Apollos, that " eloquent man and mighty in the Scriptures," and " expounded unto him the way of the Lord more perfectly." And coming down to later times who was Peter Boehler? A name almost unknown to the world, it is replied; but he was the man whom God used to prepare John Wesley for his prodigious work. This is not according to human wisdom indeed; but have we never read in Scripture that " those members of

the body which seem to be more feeble are necessary "?   The Church in all ages has had her lamp-
lighters, whose calling it has been to kindle with
Pentecostal fire those who were ordained to shine
illustriously, holding forth the word of life.   They
have lighted these candles of the Lord, and then
have themselves stepped back into obscurity and
been forgotten by their generation.*   But their
reward will be great of our Father which is in.
heaven, and they should be esteemed very highly
by us for their work's sake.

And how may those *fruits* of the Spirit on
which we have dwelt—communion, peace, holiness, and power—be acquired ?   We shall answer
again : not so much by seeking them directly and
for themselves, as by seeking that Holy Spirit in
whom they are all contained, and from whose indwelling fulness they are certain to result.

The joy of communion, for example, will be

---

* It would be most interesting to trace this principle in its application to obscure sects, in their mission of illuminating and quickening the
great Church of God—Friends of God, Poor men of Lyons, Moravians,
Quakers, Mystics, Brethren, etc.   These sects, though little among the
tribes of Judah, building no splendid churches, fashioning no stately
rituals, have yet powerfully influenced the spiritual life of the generations
to which they have belonged.   We may mention especially the
"United Brethren," and their influence in bringing the light to such
eminent servants of God as Wesley and Tholuck and Hengstenberg ;
we may mention also the "Brethren" of our day, who, while greatly
perplexing the Churches by their disorganizing theories of ecclesiastical
order, have yet been wonderfully used of God in relighting that torch
of Primitive Christianity, the Hope of Christ's Personal and Premil-
lennial Advent, and reviving clear and simple views of the doctrine of
justification by Christ's work for us.

quite certain to elude us, if we are too intent on
obtaining it for itself. It will come to us, if at
all, as the outcome of service rather than as the
income of meditation. Tauler gives the true
counsel, and such as will apply to every age and
to every Christian — " When you are plunged in
interior meditation, and God calls you to go forth
and preach, or to discharge to some sick person a
duty of charity, do it promptly and with joy ; and
the presence of God will be more sensible to you
than as if you remain concentrated upon self."
Exercise brings the warmth and glow of health,
and he will have the truest spiritual health who
most exercises himself unto godliness., And so
with the soul's happy rest in the Lord amid trials
and perturbations. "And the peace of God that
passeth all understanding *shall keep your hearts
and minds."* Ah ! blessed promise ; we have not
to keep the peace ; God's peace keeps us. The
sick man is struggling to retain his breath and
keep his hold upon the vital air ; but the well man
lets the air keep him ; it surrounds and encom-
passes and maintains him, and he rests in it without a thought of trying to keep it. Thus, O soul,
rest in God's peace until the God of peace shall
sanctify you wholly. And even holiness may not
be sought so much directly as by the worship and
service of a holy God. Looking to Jesus shows
us our sins, but it also assimilates us to His perfection. Let us look at what He is then. Contem-

plating our holiness for sanctification is as fatal an
error as gazing on our sins for justification.   He
that humbles himself shall be exalted.   It is when
John the Baptist is saying, " He must increase but
I must decrease," that his Lord is saying, " Among
them that are born of woman there hath not arisen
a greater than John the Baptist."   God's estimate
of our holiness will be according to our estimate
of our sin and unworthiness.   And holiness has no
value except as measured by God's rule.

And after all that we have said, we must once
more enforce the caution that none make these
inner experiences, which we have detailed, their
model.   God has predestined us " to be conformed
to the image of His Son," not to the experience of
our brethren.   That image is alone unchangeable
amid all human mutations.   Our spiritual state lies
often in extremes ; now the mount of transfigura-
tion and the vision of the Lord in glory ; and next
the valley of suffering with the lunatic's cry, and
the Master's rebuke, " Oh, faithless and perverse
generation ! "   From highest exaltation to deepest
spiritual depression is the frequent history of God's
servants.   Therefore let us fasten to no human
model, but rather hold our eyes ever upon Him
" who is the image of the invisible God."   An affectionate disciple of Charles Simeon has recorded
how he learned this lesson.   Once Simeon was
found " so absorbed in the contemplation of the
Son of God, and so overpowered with a display of

His mercy to his soul, that, full of the animating theme, he was incapable of pronouncing a single word, only, after an interval breaking forth with accents of " Glory ! glory ! glory ! "   The young disciple said to himself at once, " I have known nothing of such fervours as this ; and what right have I to believe that I am a Christian, or that I love the Lord at all ? "   He almost shrank from going to his accustomed meeting with his spiritual teacher, so unworthy did he feel.   He went, however, and to his surprise found Simeon so bowed in contrition and humiliation that he could only cry out, " My leanness, my leanness ! " and with smiting of his breast utter the publican's prayer.   " Now I perceived," says the disciple, " that God dispenses His favours when and how He pleases ; that He suits His dispensations to our several states and wants, and that the safest method we can take is to be sober and vigilant and to watch unto prayer."   Yes, verily !   " These wait all upon Thee, that Thou mayest give them their meat *in due season*."   He who is our spotless offering and exemplar is also our holy food ; and He imparts Himself to us when He will and how He will.   But this much we know, that " they that seek the Lord shall not want any good thing." Recur again to the scene of Christ's sealing, and ponder the lesson which it teaches.   " Labour not for the meat which perisheth," He says, " but for that meat which endureth unto everlasting life, which the Son of man shall give unto you, *for Him hath God the Father sealed.*" When the lamb was brought forward for sacrifice in the Jewish worship, it must be certified to be without spot before it could be offered ; therefore the priest was required to examine it, and, if he found it without blemish, to seal it with the temple seal.   On the banks of the Jordan, God's Lamb was sealed with the signet of the Father and certified by the Holy Ghost. Now John the Baptist, looking on Him who was to be lifted on the cross, could say, " Behold the Lamb of God which *taketh away the sin of the world* " ; and afterwards that other John, looking up to the Father's right hand, could say, " The Lamb in the midst of the throne *shall feed them.*" The spotless sacrifice of God and the holy food of God!   On the one our assurance of justification can rest for ever, because God's righteousness there rests for ever : in the other our spiritual hunger can find constant satisfaction, because God's holiness there finds constant satisfaction.   In the Lamb on Calvary who " offered Himself without spot to God," we have Christ's all-sufficient work *for us :* from the Lamb in glory giving His flesh " for the life of the world," we have His all-sufficient work *in us.*   Over our Redeemer's work for us we see it written, " It is finished " ; concerning His work in us we find it written, " Being confident of this very thing, that He which hath begun a good work in you will perform it until the day of Jesus Christ."